WHITETAIL SECRETS
VOLUME THREE

SCRAPE HUNTING FROM A to Z

J. WAYNE FEARS

DERRYDALE PRESS

Lyon, Mississippi

WHITETAIL SECRETS

VOLUME THREE, SCRAPE HUNTING FROM A to Z

Published by the Derrydale Press, Inc. under the direction of:

Douglas C. Mauldin, President and Publisher

Craig Boddington, Series Editor

Sue Goss Griffin, Series Manager

Lynda Bell Taylor, Administrator

David Baer, Illustrator

Kirby J. Kiskadden, Designer

Cover: color photo by Charles J. Alsheimer

Frontispiece: J. Wayne Fears with a Fine Whitetail.

Frontispiece photo by J. Wayne Fears

Copyright © November 1994 by Derrydale Press, Inc.

Inquiries should be addressed to the Derrydale Press, Inc., P.O. Box 411, Lyon, Mississippi 38645, Telephone 601-624-5514, Fax 601-624-3131

Library of Congress Catalog Card Number: 94-69736

ISBN 1-56416-153-6

2 4 6 8 9 7 5 3 1

Printed in the United States of America
on acid-free paper.

DEDICATION

For Tatiana and Taylor the next generation
of conservationists.

TABLE OF CONTENTS

EDITOR'S FOREWORD

The author of this, our third volume of WHITETAIL SE-CRETS, should certainly be no stranger to America's white-tail hunters. For the last many years his work has graced the pages of most of America's hunting and shooting maga-zines, and he is the author of fully 14 books on hunting and the outdoors. This is an impressive body of work for any one writer, but J. Wayne Fears has done much more than just put words on paper. He was one of the first of the Army's elite Special Forces, training and experience which, to this day, make him a leading authority on woodcraft and survival. He is a trained and accredited wildlife biologist, and he spent many years as a guide and outfitter literally across North America. These diverse qualifications make J. Wayne Fears unique in the sphere of American hunting and gunwriters—but, for our purposes, what is most im-portant of all is that J. Wayne Fears, like so many millions of American hunters, is first and foremost a whitetail fa-natic. It's also worth mentioning that his wife, Sherry K. Fears, is a serious hunter herself as well as a very successful public relations agent in the shooting and hunting indus-try. Together they're one of the top teams in the business today.

As a magazine editor I've worked with J. Wayne Fears' manuscripts before, so I knew this book would be well thought out, well-organized, well-written, authoritative, and enjoyable. It was all these things for me, and it will be for you. Although I've known Wayne for years around the show circuit and at writers' gatherings, I've spent little time with him until fairly recently, when we shared a stint on the National Rifle Association's Great American Hunters Tour. Now I can say from first-hand knowledge that not only is J. Wayne Fears all the things I've just said—he's also a really super guy and a great companion. Like most of you, I haven't had the pleasure of hunting with J. Wayne Fears. But I'd like to—and, as you can now, I've enjoyed hunting with him through the pages of this book!

Scrape hunting is his personal favorite hunting technique, and was his choice for his initial contribution to this series. Like many experienced whitetail hunters, he understands what scrapes can do for him as a hunter. But as a wildlife biologist, he can shed additional light on what scrapes are really all about. And as a master woodsman and longtime guide, he is uniquely qualified to help us take advantage of this most significant signpost of the whitetail rut!

So sit back and enjoy *SCRAPE HUNTING FROM A to Z*—and get ready to put some of those secrets to use this fall. I certainly will!

Craig Boddington
Lakewood, Colorado
August 21, 1994

CHAPTER 1

INTRODUCTION TO SCRAPE HUNTING

If you described your dream whitetail deer hunt, you would probably be hunting a deer that left calling cards so you would know where to find it. The deer you were hunting would be the dominant one in the woods, of course, and it could reasonably be expected to happen by at any time of the day. Best of all, it would abandon at least some of its usual caution and make mistakes that would improve your chances of scoring a hit.

Sound like fantasyland? Maybe not, if you're scrape hunting.

To many hunters, the term "scrape hunting" simply means taking a stand where you can see several scrapes and waiting for a buck to check them out. But that isn't the only nor always the best method of hunting in the vicinity of scrapes.

During the past 30 years I have been scrape hunting, I have taken many large bucks throughout the whitetail range by sitting in blinds or stands within view of scrapes, hunting corridors leading to scrapes, rattling or calling near scrapes, and ambushing traveling bucks in the vicinity of their scrapes. All these hunting techniques relate to scrapes.

I didn't always know about scrape hunting, and during those years I only took young bucks that you certainly couldn't call trophies. It wasn't until I finished college and moved to south Georgia to work as a wildlife specialist with the University of Georgia Cooperative Extension Service that I happened upon a woods-wise wildlife manager who gave me my first lesson in scrape hunting.

Knowing when, where, and how to scrape hunt can help you take the largest buck of your life.

I was hunting the flat, pine-palmetto woods west of the Okefenokee Swamp. After several days of not even seeing a deer, I was ready to give up.

J. Lee Rentz, then manager of the Suwannoochee Wildlife Management Area, recognized that I was having trouble hunting this swampy terrain that was new to me. "Get into my truck," he told me. "I'm going to teach you how to deer hunt." I knew he had spent many years working with deer, so I welcomed the opportunity to learn.

"The most predictable thing we know about whitetail bucks is that they are unpredictable," he began as we rode into the game management area. "I only know of one thing that bucks do consistently enough for hunters to rely on, and that's work scrapes," he continued. "I'm sure they didn't teach you college boys much about buck scrapes in school, but no matter where you find whitetail bucks, they work scrapes, and scrape hunting will get you a good buck."

We continued riding until we reached the edge of an area that had recently been clearcut. Leaving the truck, we started walking along the edge where the clearcut and the adjacent uncut woods met. We immediately started finding fresh rubs on the small saplings growing next to the woods. I was getting excited, but J. Lee kept walking. Suddenly he stopped. Pointing to a scraped-out spot in the sandy soil about two feet in diameter, J. Lee told me to smell the dirt. Stooping, I picked up a handful of the fresh dirt and sniffed; it had the strong smell of urine.

"Look up," he instructed.

About four feet above the scrape, the overhanging bushes were broken and shredded.

"This is the sure sign of a mature buck," J. Lee continued. "If you follow the edge of this clearcut, you will probably find several more of these scrapes. During the rut, a buck will stake out his territory by arbitrarily making

An elevated stand is generally, though not always, the best way to take advantage of a scrape. (Photo by Judd Cooney)

Early the next morning, I sprinkled deer lure on my boots and eased into the thicket to squirt lure in each of the three nearby scrapes. Then I selected a downwind tree some 25 yards away for my portable tree stand. I waited all day. Late that afternoon, I heard a noise that sounded like a wounded elephant coming through the thicket. It was a nice eight-point buck. He was grunting, pawing, and fighting bushes with his antlers, all at the same time. Three arrows later, he waved his tail goodbye to me and crashed, unharmed, over a sand dune. I didn't take home any venison, but I believed in scrape hunting more than ever.

My introduction to scrape hunting was many years ago, and I have spent each hunting season since trying to learn more about this fascinating method of hunting, as well as passing along what I've learned to fellow hunters.

Sometimes you don't have to pass along too much information, maybe just where some scrapes are located, for a hunter to enjoy the magic of scrape hunting. Several years ago, I was stuck in the office during the last week of the Alabama deer season. It was a cold, but beautiful, January morning, and I knew it was the peak of the rut where I hunted. I was having trouble keeping my mind on work.

The ringing telephone awakened me from my daydream. An excited voice was on the other end of the line.

"I got him, a big nine-pointer! He came right to the scrapes you told me about yesterday. You put me right on him!"

It was John Patterson, a friend I had enjoyed several hunts with. The morning before, John had driven from his home in Lincoln, Alabama, over to Tuscaloosa to hunt with me on my hunting lease. Work intervened, and I was unable to get away for the hunt. I told John where I had located several fresh scrapes and suggested a particular tree where he might best take a stand, provided the wind was cooperating.

Since John did not know the area very well, it was after daylight when he found the scrapes we had discussed the day before. He cautiously walked up to the largest scrape, squirted a few drops of deer lure into it, and moved out some 30 yards to a downwind stand to wait. The wait was short. Within an hour, John took the largest deer of his life with one shot.

Though not always so, scrape hunting can be as easy as Patterson's hunt, and it will work whether you are hunting in Texas, Montana, New York, or Florida, provided you do a number of things right.

But scrape hunting can be much more challenging. Wind and scent are always considerations, and you may even need to make your own mock scrapes. If you want to speed up a buck's coming to a scrape, you can use his super sense of hearing by calling or rattling in some circumstances. Since some techniques don't always work, you should know when to change your methods and have an arsenal of tactics to try.

All of those skills and more follow. Knowing when, where, and how to scrape hunt can help you take the largest buck of your life.

CHAPTER 2

UNDERSTANDING THE RUT

While most deer hunters think of "the rut" simply as a few days or a few weeks during which the deer in an area are breeding, a number of phases lead up to and follow that peak period. All of these phases involve sexual activities that are part of the rutting process.

This entire process takes place over a three- to four-month period, usually shorter in the North and longer in some areas of the South. Pre-rut activities may begin as early as August in some areas, and the rut may not end in other areas until as late as February.

The most important fact to learn about when rutting activities occur is that the period varies from place to place, as well as from year to year, even within the same state. When you read or hear, as I have, that the rut occurs everywhere during the second week of November, or at any other specific time, you would be wise to doubt your source's experience. It just doesn't happen that way.

You should also be aware that much of what is being reported as fact is actually theory. We simply don't have all the answers about why deer do what they do or when they do it.

Bucks are capable of breeding at any time after they've shed their antler velvet. Older bucks shed their velvet first. Biologists have identified four stages of sexual activity following and leading up to the period when most does are breeding, or the peak of the rut.

During the sparring stage of the rut, bucks push one another around with their antlers.

Prior to the chasing stage of the rut, bucks tend to stay in groups, seldom mixing with does.

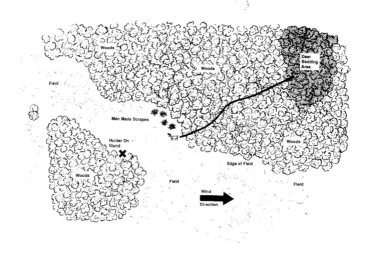

Sparring Stage

As summer gives way to fall, bucks are still in buck groups. After they shed their velvet, bucks begin having sparring matches. These aren't fights to the death or anything resembling that. They simply push one another around with their antlers. Younger bucks tend to spar more than the older bucks. During this stage, bucks pay little attention to does.

These sparring matches help bring on what many hunters consider a sign of the rut—"swollen" necks in bucks. While in the past the visibly enlarged necks of bucks were thought to be the result of glandular changes during the rut, most biologists now accept the theory that bucks' neck muscles are enlarged by the sparring and rubbing activities.

Bucks begin to make rubs during this stage.

The senses of a mature whitetail buck are so keen as to render him nearly bulletproof. The rut gives the hunter the only real advantage he is likely to attain. (Photo by Judd Cooney)

Chasing Stage

Some two to eight weeks after bucks begin sparring, the chasing stage sets in. Mature bucks leave the buck groups and, traveling alone, begin to follow does. During this time, does are producing pheromones as the estrus nears, and, perhaps in response, male hormone production increases in bucks.

At first, bucks follow the does at some distance, as the females, not yet ready for breeding, will not permit the bucks to get too close. Early in this stage, bucks will abandon the chase within a short distance, 200 to 500 yards. While several bucks may trail one doe, it is the dominant buck that follows closest.

As the doe nears her estrus, commonly referred to as being "in heat," the chase becomes more intense. When two mature bucks chasing the same doe cross paths, vicious fights may occur. It is these fights that hunters try to imitate by rattling.

Scrape hunting is one of the best ways to get the drop on a mature whitetail buck! (Photo by Judd Cooney)

As a doe gets nearer her estrus, the chase speeds up. A buck will stay on her trail longer, often for hours. After she stops to urinate, the buck may stop at this same place and sniff the urine. When doing so, he may lift his head and curl his upper lip back in what is known as the flehmen posture. It is thought that he is testing the doe's nearness to estrus when he goes through this act.

During the chasing stage, bucks continue making rubs and start to make scrapes throughout their range. In areas where the buck-to-doe ratio is close, bucks not chasing does may check their scrapes often and at all hours. A doe which is nearing estrus and is not being chased by a buck may urinate in a fresh scrape she comes across. If the estrus is very near, she may stay close to a fresh scrape until the buck returns. It is just nature's way of getting two consenting adults together.

In a heavily-hunted area where does are abundant, the role of rubs and scrapes will have less value. Rubs and especially scrapes will be fewer in number, as bucks will have little trouble finding all the girlfriends they can handle. This is not a good situation for the scrape hunter who likes to sit on a stand and wait for a buck to come work his scrapes. It could be a long wait.

In more open country of the western states, there may also be a shortage of scrapes in some areas. Bucks can see does at a long distance, so there is little need to make lots of scrapes to meet a doe.

As the chasing stage reaches its peak, bucks urinate on their tarsal glands, located on the inside of the hind legs, while rubbing the legs together. Often they will do this while working their scrapes. It produces an odor so strong that hunters can sometimes smell it at a distance. Biologists think this act is to attract does, as well as to intimidate other bucks.

Tending Stage

Just prior to the estrus period, a doe will allow the buck that's been chasing her to get close without running. During this short period just before breeding, he stands near her rear, testing her readiness to mate. Where she goes, he goes. This stage usually lasts for a few hours.

Breeding Stage

The estrus period, usually lasting about 24 hours, finally arrives. The doe will now stand for the buck to mount her. After breeding the doe, the buck will stay with her throughout her estrus period, running other bucks away. The pair will mate several times during their short stay together.

In a well-balanced deer herd, all bucks may go through the chasing stage, but it will be the older, dominant bucks that will tend and breed the does. Younger bucks will be forced to wait until they are in the $3^1/_2$ or older age class before they can participate in the actual breeding.

In a heavily-hunted deer herd where there are few older bucks, many of the younger bucks will breed does.

After the doe completes her estrus period, the buck that has been with her will again check his scrapes to locate another doe coming into estrus. He will most likely breed several does in a short period of time.

A doe that does not become pregnant during her first estrus will come into heat again in approximately 28 days. If she fails to become pregnant the second time, she will go into estrus in another 28 days. Deer researchers have found that some does repeat the estrus cycle up to seven times. However, a high percentage of does do become pregnant during their first estrus cycle.

It is the few does that repeat the estrus period that excite bucks into reworking their scrapes almost a month later.

Several years ago, I hunted a nice, 10-point buck on a farm in South Carolina. After sitting on four freshly-worked scrapes for two days, the buck showed up late the second afternoon. As he approached one of the scrapes, I watched him through my riflescope, waiting for the shot I wanted. He had a distinguishing white patch of hair on the left side of his neck.

As he slowly approached the scrape, I eased the rifle safety off and took a deep breath. At that same moment, a doe stood up to my left, and the buck bolted and ran. I didn't get off a shot.

I checked the scrapes for the next four weeks, and they weren't touched. In fact, they were filled with leaves. Then one morning as I was walking back to my truck from another stand, I checked the scrapes to find they were freshly worked and smelled like an outhouse.

My schedule didn't allow me to hunt the scrapes the next few days, so I told a friend about them. The next morning, he came by my office to show me the 10-pointer with the white spot on its neck.

Evidently, a doe came into her second estrus and got the buck interested again.

When I was the wildlife manager for a large paper company in southwestern Alabama, I saw bucks return to scrapes and work them as late as February and early March. No doubt, some does in that area didn't become pregnant until their second or third estrus. Had that occurred during the deer season, a scrape hunter would have had three good opportunities to hunt fresh scrapes.

Length of the Normal Rutting Process

To illustrate how the stages of sexual activity occur, let's look at an area where the peak of the rut is around November 14. Bucks would shed their velvet around the last of August and the first week of September, then go into the sparring stage about September 7. During the next three to four weeks, they will make many rubs.

Around October 1, the chasing stage will get underway and the first scrapes will appear. By November 1, there will be many fresh scrapes. Starting about the third week of October, some tending and breeding will occur, with the majority taking place between November 10 and November 18. Following that, all mating activity comes to a halt until those does that didn't become pregnant on their first cycle come into their second estrus. This activity will not be as pronounced as the first rut and will take place around mid-December.

Prime Time

By now it should be obvious that the prime time to scrape hunt is the three weeks prior to the peak of the rut. It's during that time that bucks are actively looking for does by working scrapes, traveling at all hours, coming to calls, and, in general, making the mistakes that allow us to get a shot. It's not the period of the greatest amount of breeding that offers the best hunting. At that point, most of the larger bucks are with does and taking care of business.

Researchers are constantly studying the rutting process, and we continue to learn more about this interesting period in a whitetail's year. Anyone who is a serious scrape hunter would do well to continue to learn everything possible about the deer's rut and to consider every theory.

CHAPTER 3

WHAT IS A RUB & WHAT DOES IT MEAN?

During the early stages of the rut, mature bucks begin leaving a sign that stirs the blood of any deer hunter—rubs on trees. These take on many forms, depending on where you hunt, the number of deer in the area, the buck:doe ratio, and the age of the bucks.

In deer herds with large numbers of older bucks, you will find more rubs than in areas where the buck population is mostly younger, say, 1½ to 2½ years old. Where there is a shortage of suitable trees for rubbing, bucks might rub a fence post or power pole. Bucks have been known to rub metal fence posts.

Why bucks make rubs as the rutting process starts is not fully understood, but it is believed to have to do with the deer's communication system. The forehead skin contains glands, called tubular apocrine sudoriferous glands, that become more active during the rut and leave a scent on the objects rubbed. Both bucks and does are known to mark buck rubs with their foreheads. Scent left on rubs persists for several days.

What Size Buck Made That Rub?

The question most asked about rubs is, "Are big rubs made by big bucks?" Research on that point is often conflicting.

During the 30 years I have been observing deer, I have seen big bucks rub saplings the size of a pencil, and I have seen them rub trees that were 12 inches in diameter. On the other hand, I have seen spikes rub trees of both those sizes. However, far more often, I have seen larger bucks rub larger trees than smaller bucks and smaller bucks rub smaller saplings than large bucks. Thus, my theory is that more often than not, big rubs are made by big bucks.

Why Do Many Small Rubs Appear in One Place?

Have you ever walked up on a ridge-top in early fall and seen 20 to 30 small rubs on saplings? Most experienced hunters have. Hunters typically have a strong urge to place a stand there to take the buck that made the rubs.

More often than not, these small rubs were made by a group of young bucks. At the beginning of the rut, bucks

One of the first lessons to learn about rubs is that lots of rubs don't necessarily mean lots of bucks.

Bucks communicate by chewing branches, rubbing their foreheads on twigs and saplings, and urinating in scrapes.

are still traveling in groups. Since most of the bucks in the typical deer population are in the younger age classes, the groups of bucks will be similarly composed. Young bucks will rub many saplings while loafing in the area. The rubs they make are not an indication that they will return to rub again or that a larger buck will be attracted to the area.

The deer hunter can also be fooled by old rubs in an area where there are no scrapes. An older buck that stays in a thicket during late summer and early fall will rub numerous saplings as he sheds his velvet and begins the early stage of the rut. On my farm is a hollow where an eight-point buck spends the summer. It has good cover, water, and lots of food. Each September you can find dozens of small saplings he has rubbed, but he moves out to another area by the time the deer season opens. It's a temptation to all who hunt with me to take a stand in the hollow with all the rubs, but it would be a waste of time.

The exact message left in a rub isn't fully understood, but we certainly understand it's one of the more important buck signs in the woods! (Photo by Judd Cooney)

There is another long hollow on my neighbor's property that a buck uses as a corridor to travel from a bedding area high on some hills planted in pine to agricultural fields. Each September, this buck rubs saplings all along the hollow as he makes his trips back and forth. The corridor is full of rubs, but they are all made by one buck.

The lesson is that lots of rubs don't necessarily mean lots of bucks.

Favorite Trees to Rub

Bucks seem to prefer specific trees to rub. One type they like to rub is aromatic trees such as cedar, pine, sassafras, and juniper. They often seem to like small saplings with a lot of spring to them, or a sapling that will "fight back." In these cases, the bucks like to rub small hickory, gallberry, willow, alder, mesquite, and oak trees.

I have followed rub lines many times when the species of the sapling rubbed didn't seem to matter. One buck I followed rubbed saplings of eight different species of trees within a half-mile. He rubbed whatever sapling he walked by that was about the diameter of an index finger.

Signpost Rubs

The type of rub that gives the deer hunter the best clue when it's time to scrape hunt is commonly called a "signpost rub" or "traditional rub." This is a large tree that bucks rub each year and return to often during the rut. Almost any species of tree may be used. A Texas rancher once showed me a six-inch creosote fence post that bucks had used so long it was rubbed almost in half, so the tree bucks choose for a signpost may simply be what's available.

Some research indicates that signpost rubs are most often found near a dominant buck's bedding area. For reasons still unknown, he likes the tree, and each year he rubs it often during the rut. As other bucks pass through the area, they smell his scent and also rub the tree.

Researchers have set up cameras on signpost rubs and recorded a number of rutting bucks, especially at night, coming to the signpost to rub. Some of these bucks were spikes, so the big rub attracted young bucks as well as older, larger bucks.

I know of two hunters who have taken nice bucks by hunting signpost rubs. They locate several and mark them on U.S.G.S. topo maps. Once the early stages of the rutting process start, they scout the signpost rubs and select one with lots of fresh sign around it. They put up a portable tree stand near the rub and wait for a buck to show up.

These hunters warn that, since the signpost rub is near the buck's bedding area, you must try not to disturb the area when you are scouting. Otherwise, you will push the buck out of his bed and cause him to come to the rub only at night.

Several research projects are ongoing to learn more about the role signpost rubs play in the rutting process. The findings of these projects should shed some light on how hunters can use these interesting rubs.

Hunting Rubs

With the exception of the two hunters mentioned above, I know of few hunters who hunt rubs with any degree of success. One notable exception is well-known deer hunter Bill Bynum of Tennessee. Bynum has taken several good bucks by making mock rubs, during periods of a new moon, and hunting them. In Bynum's opinion, early in the rut bucks bed down most of the night on dark nights and move during the daylight hours, often along their rub lines.

Bynum begins by finding a line of rubs. Between two of the rubs, he finds a suitable sapling and, using a deer

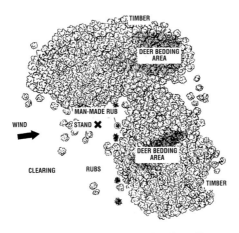

antler, makes a new rub. Next, he backs off some four feet from the sapling and puts down a few drops of buck urine. He takes a stand within bow range and waits for the buck to check the rub line. While it doesn't work every time, Bynum has taken bucks at his rubs in as little as three hours and as long as three days.

Expect the Unexpected

When scouting for rubs during the early stages of the rut, be observant for unusual rubs. Remember, bucks have been known to rub some strange things.

Several years ago I was scouting a hardwood ridge in New England. In a thickly wooded area, I came upon a stump that had obviously been rubbed many times. Hunting season wasn't yet open, so I set up a ground blind and watched the stump with my camera. The wait was short. The stump was visited four times that day by a nice buck. He would spend about five minutes each time rubbing his forehead on the stump.

We still have much to learn about rubs. As we learn more, we may find that they can be hunted much like scrapes.

CHAPTER 4

WHAT IS A SCRAPE?

If you think you know what a scrape is and there's nothing new for you to learn here, you might be well advised to read on a bit. During the years I spent guiding whitetail deer hunters and working as a deer manager, I encountered numerous hunters who thought scrapes were the rubs deer made on trees. I also saw some "scrape hunters" who spent days watching wild turkey scratchings.

First, let's determine what a scrape really is. A scrape is a bare spot of ground, ranging in size from a few inches in diameter to three feet or more, that a deer has pawed out for the purpose of communicating with other deer. A branch of a bush or tree will be hanging from three to six feet above the pawed-out area. It may be so high that a deer must stand on its hind legs to reach it with its mouth.

While it is primarily bucks that make scrapes during the early stages of the rutting process, not all bucks make scrapes. And, some does make scrapes.

A scrape made by a mature buck is loaded with scent. The pawed-out area is scented with urine, which has often run over the tarsal glands on the buck's legs. Sometimes he deposits droppings in the scrape. The buck chews on the overhanging limb and rubs his forehead glands and sometimes his eyes on it.

The Purpose of Scrapes

During the earliest stage of the rut, a scrape may serve no purpose. Often referred to as a "false scrape," it is not revisited. Active scrapes made by a dominant buck are visited often prior to and during the breeding period to attract does and to let other bucks know of his presence. These are the scrapes that scrape hunters want to find. Unfortunately, there's no sure way to tell false scrapes from active ones without watching them for a period of time to see if they're worked again. If you've seen other signs that the rut is underway, you can probably assume that any fresh scrapes you find are active. Otherwise, they may be false scrapes.

A fresh scrape will be free of leaves, grass, etc. and will have a strong urine smell.

The branch overhanging a scrape will be chewed and broken. (Photo by Judd Cooney)

For several days prior to the breeding of does, the dominant buck may check out his scrapes every few hours, hoping to find a receptive doe in waiting. He will freshen them with his scent upon each visit. The scrapes will also attract other bucks which will freshen them. Deer biologist Larry Weishuhn has told me about one scrape he watched

Often a line of scrapes will be found along an old logging road such as this one.

in Texas where 13 different bucks visited the scrape during one day. Several of those bucks had large bodies and antlers and were what Weishuhn considered dominant bucks. None of the bucks showed up at the same time. They all freshened the scrape. That year, that was his most productive site for rattling antlers. In fact, he seldom failed to rattle up at least one buck around that scrape.

A doe nearing estrus will also visit active scrapes. She will freshen the scrape and either stand around the scrape for long periods or bed down near it—a pleasant surprise to the next buck working the scrape.

A buck checking his scrapes doesn't always walk right up to the scrape to see if a doe is waiting or if another deer has freshened the scrape. Often he will approach the area of the scrape from a downwind direction where he can smell it. If there is no fresh scent in the air, he will ease off. This is why the scrape hunter should always wear a cover scent and always stay alert to what is going on in the woods around him.

How Many Scrapes Does a Buck Make?

How many scrapes a buck makes can vary from none to many. It's unclear why some bucks never make a scrape. Some make numerous scrapes, while, under certain circumstances, others make few.

In open country, such as in the whitetail range of the western states, some bucks seldom make scrapes because they can visually locate does and other bucks at a distance, eliminating the need for scrapes.

Bucks also make few scrapes in areas with overpopulated deer herds, especially where most bucks are 2 1/2 years old or younger. They have little difficulty locating does, and they have all they can handle.

The best scrape hunting is in thick cover where deer populations are under the carrying capacity of the habitat and where the buck:doe ratio is narrow. These bucks have to work to locate a receptive doe. They make lots of scrapes, often referred to as lines of scrapes, and check them often.

As the buck searches the area for does approaching estrus, he may abandon scrapes in one location and create new ones in another. A few days later, he may return to the original scrapes and reopen them. This is the reason it takes time and patience to sit on scrapes when hunting.

Where To Look For Scrapes

A whitetail buck has very definite ideas about where to make scrapes. He likes his scrapes in areas where does are likely to encounter them while on the move. He likes to put them in more open areas where he can easily see if a doe is near the scrapes. It has been my experience that the soil type influences where scrapes are made. When they have a choice, bucks seem to prefer loose soils, such as sandy loam, that are easy to paw out.

I have found scrapes throughout the whitetail range in very predictable locations, such as edges of agricultural fields, food plots, pastures, clearcuts, and old abandoned homesites. These are often the same areas in which does are feeding. Along open creekbottoms, on open ridgetops, and in open areas in thick woodlands are good spots to find scrapes. Trails and narrow corridors used by deer are sometimes used by bucks to lay down a line of scrapes.

A fresh scrape will smell of urine—but use caution when checking; you don't want to contaminate it with your own scent. (Photo by Judd Cooney)

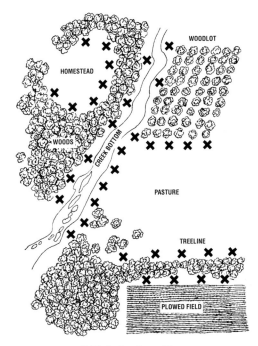

X=Likely place to scout for scrapes.

Record Scrape Locations

The ideal location for a buck to make a scrape is limited in some areas, and he or another buck will make scrapes in the same place year after year. Weishuhn has seen scrapes made in the same spot for six consecutive years in his home state of Texas. I have seen scrapes under the same tree in Alabama for eight straight years.

In other states, I have found fresh scrapes in the same location where years earlier I hunted over scrapes.

The serious scrape hunter should record all scrapes on a U.S.G.S. topo map for future use. It will become a prized possession.

CHAPTER 5

THE SCRAPE HUNTER'S GUIDE TO SCOUTING

As I was writing this chapter, I was discussing the subject with a friend who is an avid scrape hunter. "All you need to tell them is to find some fresh scrapes and go hunting," was his advice to me.

While it sounds simple, there is much more to it than that. The scrape hunter must have the scouting skills of a master deer hunter if he is to be successful on a regular basis. The more he knows about the deer in the area he plans on hunting, the easier it will be for him to find scrapes and know how to hunt them. Just going out on the chance of finding scrapes to set up on is a poor way of hunting.

The savvy scrape hunter scouts year-round. He records notes of his findings on a U.S.G.S. topographical map. Some signs such as trails, bedding areas, and scrapes occur at the same place at the same time each year. I hunt several areas where bucks make scrapes in the same locations every year. Thanks to my maps, I can go back to these same scrape locations anytime I'm hunting the area during the rut.

There's a low-hanging dogwood tree at the edge of an abandoned field on a friend's farm where I've taken nice bucks on four separate occasions. Year after year, bucks return to the same location to make scrapes.

Pre-rut scouting helps you find areas with a huntable population and helps you learn the lay of the land. Scouting during the rut helps you use the information you gathered during the pre-rut trips to locate rubs, scrapes, corridors of travel, creek crossings, and other strategic points of travel.

Post-season scouting can be the most thorough of all, as you're no longer being cautious not to spook deer, and, perhaps most importantly, you don't stop to hunt when you find promising sign. You'll likely find rubs and scrapes you didn't find during your other scouting trips, especially in secluded areas that bucks used when there was hunting pressure in the woods. Many expert scrape hunters like Larry Weishuhn and Bill Bynum consider post-season scouting to be the most valuable scouting for the next hunting season.

Scouting during the rut helps you use information learned during pre-rut scouting to locate rubs and scrapes.

Deer leave many signs, some of which tell you a great deal, while others tell you very little. However, the art of interpreting deer sign is much like solving a mystery; each sign is a clue, and it tells you something about the deer. When you find several different signs and compile their meanings, you will have the potential solution to your mystery—that is, where and how to hunt the area.

As you scout your deer hunting area and look for signs, carry a U.S.G.S. topo map with you. This map is an excellent "memory bank" on which to record your findings. By marking trails, bedding areas, feeding areas, and scrapes on the map, you will see a pattern appear right before your eyes. This pattern will tell you where to locate your stand.

Let's look at several types of deer sign and see where they are found and what they tell you.

Droppings—One sign that misleads many scrape hunters is deer droppings. To the novice, deer droppings mean deer "are here now." This may or may not be true. Let's look at a few facts.

Deer droppings come in two basic shapes, round and oblong. At first glance they look like rabbit droppings; however, rabbit droppings are smaller and much more fibrous than those of the deer. Fresh deer droppings are shiny black and moist for the first day. Older droppings are dry and have a dull appearance.

Moving deer, such as on a trail, will leave droppings scattered along the route, whereas deer standing still while feeding will leave their droppings in a pile. Fresh deer droppings are an excellent indication that deer are using the area. However, don't get excited and think that just because you've found several piles of deer droppings, the area contains a lot of deer. Wildlife biologists have found that a single deer can deposit droppings up to 12 times a day.

Tracks—The deer sign with more myth associated than any other is tracks. Many hunters think all tracks are fresh. Others think deer tracks always lead to deer, while yet others claim to be able to distinguish a buck track from a doe track. In most cases, none of these is true.

Deer tracks tell you only two things: (1) that deer have been here, and (2) how recently. Don't be misled by the number of tracks, as one deer has four feet and takes short steps, thus leaving lots of tracks. You can usually tell if tracks are fresh by the sharpness of the top edges of the track. On muddy roads, an old track may be dried out. Also, old tracks may be filled in with leaves or dirt.

Don't waste your time trying to distinguish buck tracks from doe tracks. Contrary to the opinion of many hunters, there is no difference. Large tracks or those that show the dew claws may be made just as easily by a heavy or running doe as by a buck. While tracks are an important sign, don't try to read too much into them.

Food—The presence of deer food may not be considered a deer sign by many hunters; however, I think it should be treated as a very important sign. When scouting for deer sign, watch for deer foods such as white oaks, Japanese honeysuckle, greenbrier, or a field of soybeans, wheat, or oats. These foods attract deer. When you find a deer food area, look for fresh tracks and fresh droppings. If you find these signs, you may have found an excellent area to search for scrapes during the rut, as bucks will search out does, and does are where the food is located. Mark the food area on your topo map for future reference, and look for the deer trails leading into the food area.

Beds—Beds are usually pressed-down spots in the leaves, grass, or pine straw about four feet by three feet.

Deer beds are a difficult sign to find, as well as to read once they are found. Wildlife biologists have found that bed locations vary considerably with each individual deer and are distributed widely throughout the deer's home range. On a cold, sunny day, deer like to bed down under the warm sun in a dry place, such as in a broomsedge field. During bad weather, such as cold, rainy, windy days, they like to bed in dense vegetation. Once the hunting pressure is on, you will find beds in the edge of thick brush where the buck can see danger coming and make a safe exit in one jump. During the hunting season, a deer often beds in the same general area, though not necessarily in the same bed.

Since bucks tend to make scrapes in the same location year after year, scrapes found when scouting should be recorded on a map.

Trails—A sight that excites most deer hunters is a well-worn trail, or runway, as some hunters call them. Deer trails can be aptly described as "paths of least resistance." Deer will often go around obstructions. Some trails are as long as a mile, while others, such as those across a stream or saddle, are as short as a few yards. Some are used for only a month or so, and others are known to exist for years.

Deer trails commonly begin as several faint trails, leading from bedding areas, outside the territory, etc., and come together to form a more prominent trail that leads to a favorite feeding area. As long as the food in the feeding area is available, the trail will be active. When the food supply is exhausted, the trail will be abandoned.

Many different animals make trails, so the deer hunter would do well to examine a new-found trail for fresh deer droppings and deer tracks. One year I was hunting with a youngster on his first deer hunt. The second morning he rushed into camp exclaiming that he had found a heavily-used deer trail leading from a wooded ridge down to a swamp lake. I got my rifle and followed him back to the trail. Indeed, it was being used, but not by deer. My young friend had found a trail made by beavers dragging saplings and small logs into the lake. Correctly identify the trail you find so you can spend your days watching deer trails, not beaver, cow, skunk, or fox trails.

I have a friend who scouts his new-found deer trails several days in a row before hunting. To confirm that the trail is still being used, he ties a piece of dark sewing thread across the trail some three feet off the ground between two trees. Each morning and afternoon, he checks the thread to see if it is broken. A broken thread indicates that a trail is active and approximately when it is being used.

When you find a good deer trail, mark it on your topo

map. More than likely, it will join with a bedding or feeding area you have already marked, or it may lead to other such areas. If you hunt from a tree stand, locate several good stand sites along the trail, keeping in mind that the wind may be blowing from any direction when you return. Mark these stands on your map. This will be helpful when you return before daylight.

Scouting During the Rut

You don't have to be Daniel Boone to know that the primary signs you are looking for during the rut are rubs and scrapes. The most valuable rubs will be the signpost rubs that deer return to each year. Smaller rubs on smaller saplings should also be noted, as they are good indications that you are in a buck's territory and scrapes may be located nearby.

Scrapes are the sign that excites deer hunters most. Most often found in open areas adjacent to brush and trees, scrapes are a sure sign that bucks are in the area and actively seeking does. (The full meaning of scrapes and the role they play in the rutting process is covered in Chapter Four.) All scrapes should be noted on your scouting map, not only for immediate reference, but for future hunting seasons.

Often the scrapes will take on a line configuration, thus the term "scrape line," as the buck will make a series of scrapes along an old logging road, *sendero*, edge of a field, bench in the side of a mountain, gas or power line right-of-way, etc. They may also make scrapes in secluded open areas in dense cover.

For years I hunted the site of what had once been a large sawmill in the middle of several thousand acres of thick

Scouting is probably the single most important step toward having a successful hunting trip.

timber. The two-acre sawmill site was on an open, sandy rise in what was otherwise flat, heavily-wooded country. Every year, several large bucks would congregate at this location to make their scrapes. One year I took two bucks on two consecutive mornings and passed up three more younger bucks, all working scrapes in this small opening.

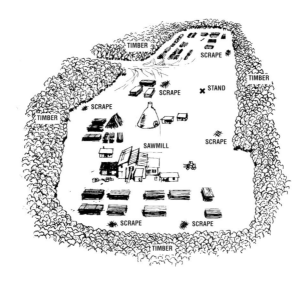

When scouting during the rut, don't overlook scouting corridors that lead from bedding areas to scrapes. Corridors with lots of rubs in them can be an ideal place to take a stand.

If the area where you hunt is heavily hunted, it's a good idea to search out secluded creek crossings, trails used by does, and doe feeding areas. You may have to change your tactics if the bucks only work their scrapes during the night. Again, be sure to record these areas on your map.

A study of your topo map will show you some good areas to scout, as corridors, thick creekbottoms, open fields, etc. show up on the map.

Post-season Scouting

When I first started guiding hunters on spring gobbler hunts, I made it a point to start scouting as soon as the deer season was over. During the month of February and the first half of March, I was in the woods looking for turkey sign and watching turkeys. The very first year I started this early, intensive turkey scouting program, I noticed something that caught me by surprise. While looking for turkey sign, I was finding an enormous amount of fresh deer sign. I was finding the hidden areas where big bucks spend the winter after the pressure of hunting season had pushed them into deep hiding.

I found two-month-old rubs and scrapes in areas that had been totally overlooked by hunters. In March, I found shed antlers. I saw heavy feeding on smilax and honeysuckle. Early that spring, I jumped bucks that still had their racks in areas so difficult to get to that I hadn't bothered to hunt there during deer season.

This sudden discovery of buck wintering grounds sparked an idea that was to be a great hunting aid the next deer season. Throughout the entire turkey scouting period and turkey season, I kept notes of my findings and sightings. By April, I had located several pockets of land that had obviously been retreats where bucks spent the winter. I planned to go into these areas during the rut the next deer season and do some intensive hunting.

The next fall, I waited until the rut and started hunting my new-found areas. The result was three nice bucks. When I was asked by my friends how I had found these deer, my answer was "post-season scouting." You can bet I got some strange looks.

To understand why post-season scouting is valuable and how to use it the following deer season, one must first understand how hunting pressure affects deer activity. In such states as Alabama and South Carolina, the deer seasons are long, and day in and day out, bucks are being hunted. Even in states or areas where the deer season is shorter, a lot of hunting pressure is brought to bear on the bucks.

Bucks, especially older ones, react to this pressure. First, many reduce their daylight-hours activity until they become almost nocturnal. This is especially true in the states with a long season. As the pressure continues and these night-traveling bucks are jumped from their hiding areas by roaming hunters, they begin to seek out areas of little or no human pressure. This can be in locations that hunters would never suspect.

At the same time that hunting pressure is causing mature bucks to move to new locations within their territory, another natural occurrence is putting pressure on them. Late in the year, the fall food crop is getting more scarce, especially during years of poor mast production. The fall crop of acorns and other nuts, soft mast, corn, soybeans, and much of the green browse play out late in the deer season. The green understory vegetation which has provided cover is disappearing.

The combination of these two natural factors causes bucks to change their diets and to seek cover. This usually means a move to areas that are thick and contain food such as smilax, honeysuckle, mushrooms, and low-growing twigs. In many cases, this is a move into moist, low areas with rich soil, such as beaver swamps, creekbottoms, and along rivers. In some cases, this can be a move to thick fence rows or woodlots adjacent to fields planted in winter pasture crops such as wheat, oats, or rye. The bucks lay up in the thick area during the day and chase does in the adjacent fields at night.

I have seen bucks move into an area of thickly-planted pines during this period. They would move out of the pines at night but hold up tight in them during the day. I have also seen them move into a thick pocket of vegetation in the middle of a clearcut. A farmer once told me that a buck stayed around his barn and silo each year and fed with his cattle. Each spring the farmer would find the buck's shed antlers, once sticking in his tractor tire. When the buck reached his peak year, the farmer couldn't resist it any longer. He shot the buck, and it almost made the book.

I don't want to give the impression that bucks go great distances to seek new hide-outs during the winter, for this is not necessarily so. They simply seek out the overlooked corners and pockets of habitat in or near their territory where cover is abundant and does are nearby. They stay in these wintering areas until the hunting pressure is gone and spring brings out an abundance of food throughout their territory. Then they move out to roam their home range. In areas where spring turkey hunting is heavy, I have seen bucks hold up in their winter hide-outs until almost summer, especially if their wintering area had an abundance of food.

Post-season scouting should begin as soon as the deer season ends. The first step is to try to find the overlooked habitat that the big bucks may have retreated to. More often than not, it will be an area that is extremely thick with low-growing vegetation. This may be a creekbottom that is thick with cane, vines, and brush. It could be an area in an old stand of planted pines where the blackberry vines are so thick that hunters are kept out. An island in a river or swamp that is thick with cover can often hold a buck or two.

In some situations, the cover doesn't have to be so thick. More open woods near buildings or in other areas that aren't hunted can be good wintering grounds. At a hunting lodge I once owned, a road makes a loop around several thousand acres of wet flatwoods. It is a mile from one side of the loop to the other. One year while post-season scouting, I found a pocket of relatively open woods in the center that was the winter home for three big bucks. During deer season, hunters had only hunted the first one-quarter mile of woods off the loop road. The center of the loop was wet

Scouting has its dangers. It's a thrill to see this buck in his bed—but spooking him from it will almost certainly cause him to change his pattern. (Photo by Judd Coney)

and muddy. No one bothered to go into the center. Since there were plenty of does and food in that area, the bucks were living the good life without being bothered by man.

To find areas such as this, try to put yourself in the place of the bucks. Where would you go to be safe, yet close to food? Answer that question and do your post-season scouting there.

Signs to look for during this period are similar to signs you would look for during a pre-season scouting trip, with an exception or two. Since the bucks—and often retreating does as well—are confined to a smaller area with thick vegetation, they will create more visible trails than they normally would. By following these trails I have often found the main wintering ground. Be observant for rubs and scrapes. In my home state of Alabama, the rut often goes on into February, and post-season scouting trips will reveal rubs and scrapes that are fresh. When you find this, be observant; you are in a buck's winter habitat. As with any scouting trip, fresh droppings and tracks can tell you that deer are using the area.

One sign I look for in the spring is dropped antlers. I do this for two reasons. Number one, an antler is a sure sign that you are in a buck's home. I mark the site where I found it on a topo map for future reference. Number two, I am always looking for dropped antlers for making rattling horns. I usually find only one antler since the buck rarely sheds both at the same time or in the same place. Only twice in my career have I found a matched pair of shed antlers in the same location. In most cases you are lucky to find one antler, as rodents are quick to gnaw on them.

Once you have found post-season sign and may possibly have seen bucks during your scouting trips, your work is complete until the next deer season. When the season opens, you can hunt the areas you regularly hunt. Save the wintering grounds for the rut.

A great way to hunt in thick areas is from a portable tree stand. By locating trails during your post-season scouting, you will have some idea where to put your portable tree stand for your late-season hunt. The secret to success when hunting from tree stands in such places is to be in the stand every chance you get. Bucks in thick wintering areas are more likely to sit about during the midday hours. Be alert at all times.

Post-season scouting has a great deal of merit, and if you are a turkey hunter, you can do two things at once. The hunter who knows where the big bucks spend the winter knows the best places to hunt undisturbed scrapes the next season.

CHAPTER 6

WIND WATCHING
IS A MUST

Carl Richardson felt confident as he took his hunting gear from his car and began the long, dark walk to his tree stand. It was a good hour before first light. He walked up a narrow valley toward the hill where he had positioned his tree stand about three-quarters of the way up the slope. From there, he'd be able to see an old logging road leading from the valley across the hill. It had numerous scrapes along its course.

The morning was cool, in the low 40's, and the humidity was high. Richardson hated getting his boots wet as he walked through the high grass in the valley.

Upon reaching his tree stand, Richardson climbed into position so he could see the scrapes toward the top of the hill. The bucks he had seen usually moved early in the morning from a feeding area on top to a dense thicket in the valley to bed.

Since there was plenty of time to kill before daylight, Richardson took his insulated bottle from his day pack and enjoyed two cups of hot coffee. As the first morning light appeared, he put away his coffee and got ready. The air seemed a bit colder, even though there didn't appear to be any wind.

The morning came and went, and again Richardson went home without a buck. It was the story of his hunting life. He had lots of scrapes to hunt, but he just couldn't seem to be at the right place at the right time.

The fact was, Richardson was defeated by the wind. He didn't know it, but almost everything he did that morning was wrong. The bucks in the darkness on the hill above his treestand knew he was there.

The Buck's Nose

To understand how to make the wind work for him, the hunter needs to understand something about a deer's sense of smell and its importance to that animal, especially during the rut.

Of all the deer's senses, the sense of smell is most acute, followed by hearing and vision, in that order. The reasons the sense of smell is so important are many. First, and perhaps foremost, the deer evolved as a woodlands animal that had to use its nose to communicate, as well as locate and identify other deer, because the dense habitat restricted visual communication.

Deer have several glands that enable the animals to communicate even when they may not be able to see one another. The tarsal gland, located on the inside of the hock, produces a scent unique to individual deer, enabling them to identify one another. It is also involved in the breeding signal. The interdigital gland, located between the hooves of deer, leaves a scent to mark a trail. The tubular apocrine sudoriferous, found in the forehead, leaves the deer's scent on trees and other objects on which it is rubbed. The preorbital gland in the inner corner of the eye serves as a tear gland, and some biologists think it is used as a signal in association with the scrape-marking activity of rutting animals. All of these activities require a strong, sensitive sense of smell.

Urine plays a major role in getting a buck and doe to-

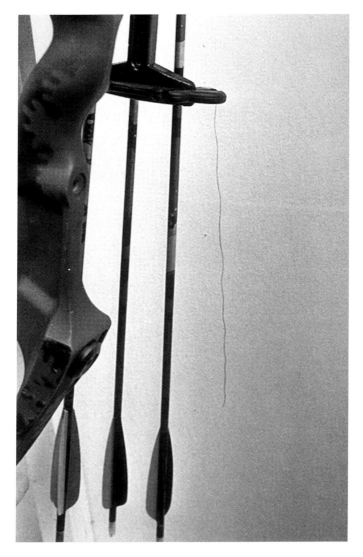

A length of sewing thread tied to the bow or upper sling swivel of a rifle allows the hunter to read the wind.

gether during the breeding season. The doe, upon finding a buck's fresh scrape, urinates in it and leaves a trail for the buck to follow. The buck uses his nose to stay on the trail until he catches up to the doe.

Hunters hunting near slopes need to understand the movement of air caused by the heating and cooling of the earth's surface.

Deer depend upon their keen sense of smell to locate food and to determine what to eat or to pass up. They sniff every bite before they consume it.

Deer depend upon their sense of smell to avoid predators, including man. Studies have shown that, in relatively open country in a gentle wind, deer can detect the odor of man for distances up to a half-mile. In a heavily-wooded area, a downwind deer can smell a hunter at one-quarter mile and pinpoint him at 200 to 300 yards with the slightest air current.

So, why is a deer's sense of smell so good? When you think of it, the answer is quite simple. The deer's nose is extremely long, when compared to man's, and it has many convoluted structures, called conchae, which are covered with tissue that is super-sensitive to odors. Since deer have many times more odor-sensory cells than man, they can detect even the slightest odors many times more easily than man.

Ongoing research also indicates that deer can use their taste buds to reinforce their sense of smell. Many hunters have seen a buck on the trail of a doe or smelling an unusual scent curl their lip—this is called the "flehmen behavior"—to place the odor in his mouth for a taste. This is a complicated process but an interesting one from which we will probably learn much more about the deer's superior sense of smell in the future.

In short, since the buck's sense of smell plays a major role in daily communication with other deer, sexual activity, food location and selection, warning of danger, and selection of travel routes, it is always on the alert and constantly tests the slightest air currents. Knowing all this, we know that to be good hunters, we must always be aware of air currents.

Far too many hunters think all they have to do is put on

some commercial cover scent to be protected from the buck's sense of smell. Far from it. While it can be a big help, we carry with us body odors and foreign odors which often override the cover scent. A buck's keen sense of smell, reinforced with its sense of taste, can often pick out the molecules of human scent from the cover scent.

Know Basic Air Movement

A common mistake made by many hunters is watching the movement of wind in tree branches to determine where to hunt. While this is better than disregarding the wind all together, there are many smaller movements of air that must also be understood.

An important air movement many hunters are not aware of is the up-slope and down-slope movement of air near the ground caused by the heating and cooling of the earth's surface. Starting fairly early in the morning as the sun heats

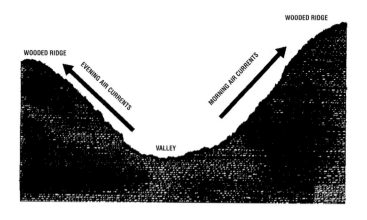

the ground, air movement is up-slope as warm air rises. In the late afternoon, as the earth's surface begins to cool, the direction of air movement has changed to down-slope. This can and should play a major role in determining where to place a stand or the direction of a stalk. For example, if you are hunting in an area with hills and valleys, you might hunt hilltops during the warm part of the day and valleys at daybreak or late in the afternoon. Knowledge of this air movement can be especially helpful when you know the bedding and feeding areas and travel routes of the deer in a specific area.

Another lesser-known air movement that can quietly carry a hunter's scent a long way usually occurs on clear days. This is the movement of air from cooler to warmer spots. As the air becomes warm and rises in a spot where the sun hits it first, a flow of cooler air is drawn from cooler spots to fill the void. How can this affect the hunter? Let's

A flag is a good wind indicator. It takes a wind speed of about 10 mph to extend the flag fully.

say a hunter has his blind in a forest adjacent to a clearcut where bucks are known to bed. As the sun warms the clearcut first, the scent of the hunter in the cooler forest is pulled into the clearcut, warning the bucks of his presence.

During periods of high humidity, human odor is stronger in the air and may be carried further distances by air currents. If there is moisture such as dew, frost, or rain-drops on vegetation, human odor is picked up easier and lingers longer on the vegetation. You should keep this in mind when walking into a stand. Try to pick a route to the stand that won't be crossed by the deer you are hunting. Also remember that long after you have walked across a damp area, air currents will be carrying your scent. Plan your route with the wind in mind.

On the stillest of days, there is an outward movement of scent from the hunter sitting on a stand. If he is in an ele-vated stand, this invisible curtain of scent will settle on the ground around the stand early in the morning and widen until air currents move it in one direction or the other. Knowing their scent is slowly moving in all directions when the air is still, many hunters would rather have a slight wind to work with when sitting on a stand than to have no air movement. Being elevated in a tree stand doesn't help in this situation. The only help is to be as odor-free as possible and to use a good cover scent.

Be Aware of Wind

A good hunter is always aware of the wind even before he leaves camp. A growing number of hunters are learning the value of having a portable weather radio in camp for con-stant reports from the local office of the National Weather Service. I use a small, battery-operated weather radio called WeatherOne. This pocket-sized radio weighs only five ounces and runs on a nine-volt battery. It gives me area wind direction and speed and other valuable weather information 24 hours a day.

Every hunting camp should have some type of wind direction indicator. At our Cross Creek Hollow hunting cabin, we fly the United States flag. The flag gives us a good idea about wind direction, direction changes, and speed. Experience has taught us that it takes a wind speed of 10 miles per hour to extend the flag fully.

In the field, the hunter can toss up a handful of dead grass or dust to get a good idea of wind direction. But this is not practical when in a tree stand or on a stand out of reach of grass or dust. Some hunters check the wind with a butane cigarette lighter or small bottle of unscented talcum powder. Both reveal even the slightest wind. However, both require motion. A better wind indicator is a length of sewing thread tied to the front swivel of the rifle, bow quiver, or upper bow limb. It is constantly at work, and you can see wind direction at a glance with no movement. It is also ideal when stalk hunting.

Rattling

One of the best deer hunters I've ever hunted with is outdoor writer/deer biologist Larry Weishuhn. He is a master at rattling up bucks. When rattling, Weishuhn watches the wind constantly and uses his knowledge of deer to set up. He sets up in a little cover where he can watch an open area downwind. He knows that many big bucks like to circle the rattling sound and run in from a downwind position. As they circle to get to this position, the hunter may get his shot. In the buck's excitement to rush in, it will

Close cover hunting usually means close encounters, where the wind becomes even more critical.

often get within range before picking up the human scent. Using the wind in this way has made Weishuhn a very successful hunter.

Hunting in High Winds

Many hunters stay in camp during periods of high winds, knowing that deer movement is limited at such times. However, this can be a productive period if you have kept notes during your scouting and know where some thickly-vegetated bottoms are located. This is a hunting technique I learned from one of Alabama's most successful deer hunters, Ken Gates.

In gusting winds, Gates moves his portable tree stand to a position looking down into thick cover growing along narrow creekbottoms. He places the stand high enough to be able to see down into the thicket and patiently waits for the rutting bucks to move. His experience has proven that bucks go into the cover to escape the high wind. Winds are calmer in the bottom, and bucks feel free to move there.

Some stalk hunters like to hunt in high winds. Hunting into the wind, their noise and movement are less notice-able, and they can sometimes catch a buck bedding or es-caping the wind in cover. I once took a mule deer buck hunting this way. A strong wind was blowing, so I moved into the wind on a rocky mesa. Easing along the tops of some high rocks, I looked down to see a nice buck stand-ing between two huge rocks, out of the wind. The 15-yard shot was easy. He never knew I was there.

Now you see why Carl Richardson never had a chance against the buck's sense of smell. The walk to his stand filled the valley with lingering human scent. The stand he selected was in a position to send human scent up the hill during the morning. His coffee was a foreign scent. Had he known about air movement, he would have planned his hunt much differently.

CHAPTER 7

SCENTS & LURES—
CRITICAL COMPONENTS
OF SCRAPE HUNTING

The buck's nose never works harder than during the rut. He is constantly on the alert for a doe in heat, and it is usually his nose that leads him to receptive ladies.

Since his nose is constantly searching for the scent of a doe, it is also informing the buck of the presence of man, more so than at any other time of the year. This is why many careless hunters sit on fresh scrapes day after day without ever seeing a buck. The rutting bucks in the area smelled the hunters and only worked the scrapes at night after the hunter had departed.

The deer hunter has two challenges related to scents when it comes to hunting scrapes. Number one, he must prevent bucks from picking up his scent, and number two, he must "sweeten up" the scrape to encourage a buck to investigate the presence of another doe. Let's look at each.

Eliminating Human Scent

It is surprising to many hunters to learn that a deer can detect human odor up to a half-mile away when the wind is blowing from the hunter to the deer. In still air, the scent is diffused in all directions and can be detected out to 100

These days there are numerous clever means to employ commercial deer scents. Most work—but only if employed properly using common sense. (Photo by Craig Boddington)

yards or more. The scents the hunter carries into the woods with him can determine just how far the deer can smell him. A hunter who wears cologne, bathes with a strong-smelling deodorant soap, or smokes cigars will obviously alarm deer at greater distances than the deer hunter who tries to eliminate all odors.

One of the most successful scrape hunters I know started out as a very unsuccessful hunter. After five years of only seeing one or two does each season, this hunter decided to get serious about improving his scrape hunting. It occurred to him one day while evaluating his past hunting trips that he often stopped at a local service station to fill up his truck with gas on the way to his hunting lease. Sometimes he would run the tank over, spilling a small amount of fuel on his boots or hands. If he didn't run the tank over, just the process of pumping gasoline got fumes on his clothing.

Back-tracking further, he realized that his mornings always began with a shower using deodorant soap, followed by a shave and liberal use of after-shave lotion. Also, his hunting clothes were being washed in a sweet-smelling detergent. In short, this hunter went into the woods smelling like a truck-stop bordello.

He immediately went about making changes in what he called his "scent-control program." He paid a few cents extra to have an attendant at the service station fill up his truck tank, or he made sure his gas tank was filled the day before. He started washing his hunting clothes in baking soda. He took his morning shower with a non-deodorant soap, and he stopped using after-shave lotion.

To complete his program, he used a commercial cover scent while hunting to cover those human scents that he had little control over, such as perspiration or breath.

The next hunting season, he was amazed at how many more deer he was seeing. Now he gets his buck each year.

As this hunter learned, the most important step in overcoming the buck's keen sense of smell is to eliminate as many human and man-made scents as possible. The next step is to use a cover scent, often called masking scent, when in the woods.

To get the most from your cover scent, you must be aware of some facts. First, regardless of how good your cover scent may be, you still must hunt with the wind in your favor, as the best cover scents won't hide all human odors. Secondly, understand that cover scents are an aid to hunting success, but not a shortcut. You still must use other skills and proven techniques. Third, many hunters think if a little cover scent is good, a lot will be great. Most experts in the field of cover scents agree that using too much cover scent is as bad as taking human scent into the woods. A strong odor has the reverse effect on deer and alarms them. In short, the value of cover scents, when used according to instructions, is to simply help put you in a rutting buck's territory without his radar-like nose detecting your presence.

The worth of cover scent was proven to me quite vividly several seasons age when I made a sudden decision during lunch to go bowhunting that afternoon. On the way out of town, I stopped at a sporting goods store and bought a bottle of red fox cover scent. When I arrived at my hunting site, I placed a few drops of the scent on my boots and on the hem of my pants. I walked several hundred yards from my car to the hardwood area I had planned to hunt. In walking into my stand, I cut across a wheat field adjacent to the woods. As I put up my portable tree stand, I noticed that the mosquitoes were out en masse, so I decided to return to my car for a bottle of insect repellent. I crossed the wheat field two more times.

At last I got settled in my tree stand for the hunt. Late that afternoon, I saw three young bucks start feeding across the wheat field. Even though they were far out of my range, I watched the bucks feed toward the path I had made in my three trips across the field. I expected them to run from the field when they crossed my path. To my surprise, they fed across the path several times with no sign of awareness that a human had crossed the field. The cover scent had done its job.

When selecting a cover scent, be sure to choose one that blends in with the natural scents found in the area you plan to hunt. If foxes or raccoons are in the area, then urine-based commercial scents of that type are good. If you are hunting around apple orchards, then use an apple scent. If you hunt around pine or cedar trees, use these scents. Using a scent that is not native to the immediate area where you are hunting is a mistake that offsets the entire principle of cover scents.

Several companies offer a variety of scent pads that are slipped on the hunter's boots. These dispensers work well, but you must remember to replenish the scent often, especially if you're walking through wet grass or hunting in wet weather.

On the subject of walking, you should remember that one of the strongest odors produced by humans is that associated with perspiration. Try to avoid working up a sweat when deer hunting, even if you are using a cover scent.

Attracting Bucks to a Scrape

A second type of scent that hunters should know the right way to use is buck lures. Several commercially-available

Taking a foreign scent, such as coffee, to your stand will alert a rutting buck several hundred yards away that you are near his scrape.

The buck's nose is his main line of defense. To be successful, you must defeat this.

buck lures, primarily urine-based, take advantage of the fact that bucks use their keen sense of smell to locate does during the rut. Most experts agree that buck lures should only be used during the rut, as their use during other periods can alarm deer. Manufacturers of deer scents recommend that the hunter use a cover scent when moving around in the woods and when on a stand during non-mating periods. Use a buck lure to pull in a buck to a specific spot when the mating season is on.

One of the major problems many hunters have had with buck lure is expecting too much from the product. You cannot expect to be successful by simply going out in the woods and hanging up a few cotton balls soaked in buck lure. For best results, buck lure should be used at scrapes. Because scent at scrapes plays such an important role in communication between bucks and does during the rut, it makes sense that a buck lure would stand a good chance of attracting a buck in this setting.

Once scrapes are located, select a stand site downwind. Wear cover scent upon entering the area, and once your stand site is selected, go to the scrape and squirt a few drops of buck lure in it. Next, hang a small scrap of cloth (I like to use flannel for this) or a commercial scent dispenser about five feet high in a bush near the scrape. Put a few drops of buck lure on the cloth to get the scent into the air more quickly. Then get on your stand and stay alert. Remember that rutting bucks move at all hours and often make a sound like a hog grunting.

Buck lure also works well in association with rattling. I like to squirt a few drops of buck lure on cotton balls and carry them in a plastic, 35mm film canister. When a rattling site near scrapes is selected, I place the cotton balls on bushes near my stand.

Collect Your Own Attractant

I like to collect my own attractant scent by *carefully* removing the deer's bladder while field dressing an animal and emptying the urine into a plastic bag or jar. Store it in the freezer until your next hunting trip. When it's needed, thaw it and put it into a small bottle with a dropper cap. This makes using the foul-smelling urine easy. Be sure to mark the bag or sack well so you won't rush to the freezer to get some soup stock and use deer urine instead.

If you don't want to store urine in your freezer, you can

preserve it for about 12 months by mixing one ounce of Benzyl Benzoate, available from trapping supply houses, to each pint of deer urine.

Which Scents and Lures Are Best?

The question that is perhaps asked the most often about cover scents and buck lures is, "Which ones are best?" I asked this same question to a number of scent manufacturers, deer biologists, and successful deer hunters. Their answers were all about the same. First, if possible, find out which scents and lures are working best with successful deer hunters who hunt in the same area you do. If this is not possible, buy two or three scents that you think would best work in your area at that time of year and try them out. Granted, this process does take time and involves extra expense, but the long-term results are worth the effort.

In the case of cover scents, you should learn all you can about what scents are likely to be native in the hunting area before making a purchase. For example, are there apple or cedar trees, foxes or skunks?

Manufacturers of scents and lures tell me that many hunters ruin the effectiveness of the product by not properly storing it. It should be stored with the cap on tight. When exposed to air for long periods of time, many scents and lures lose their strength. Also, most manufacturers recommend that you not store your cover scent or lure in a hot area or in the sun, as this will weaken the product. I've seen many hunters put on cover scent before leaving their vehicles, then toss the bottle onto the dashboard to sit in the sun all day. Keep your scents and lures in a cool, shaded location for longer life.

Several manufacturers have told me that most scents and

There is no question but that commercial scents work—but they must be natural to the area where they are used. (Photo by Judd Cooney)

lures have a life of about one year when properly stored. They recommend that hunters replenish their supply of scents and lures each year to assure that they are going into the woods with product that is strong enough to do a good job.

Never before have hunters had such a wide variety of cover scents and lures available to them in their local stores. Use some common sense in sorting through manufacturers' claims. Then heed the advice of successful hunters, do a little field-testing, and carefully follow the instructions packed in commercial scents and lures. Today's hunters can do a lot to fool the nose of ol' mossy horns.

CHAPTER 8

BASIC SCRAPE HUNTING

Most trophy hunters agree that the most productive way to hunt big, rutting bucks in an undisturbed area where the buck-to-doe ratio is reasonably low is by basic scrape hunting. Throughout this book it is mentioned that under the right conditions, a rutting buck trying to locate a doe will check his scrapes often. All you have to do is be there and shoot straight. It sounds simple, and, under the right circumstances, it actually is.

Know When the Rut Is Occurring

Regardless of where you plan to hunt scrapes, be it Montana or Maine (provided the season is open), you must hunt them during the rut. If you don't know when the rut is, call a wildlife biologist or conservation officer who lives and works in the area. They are usually glad to share this information.

Don't assume that the rutting dates for deer in one area of a state apply to all areas. Every year I read articles about the January rut in my home state of Alabama. The fact is, that's the rutting date for only one section of the state. In other parts of the state, the rut may be occurring from late October until February. The same principle applies in many other states.

Also, don't overlook the fact that all does aren't bred the first time they come into estrus; the area you hunt may have two or more peak rutting dates during which you can hunt scrapes. A biologist can share a lot of valuable information like this if you will take the time to give him a call.

The bottom line: To be successful at finding scrapes that are being used and have a chance at seeing a buck at the scrapes, the rut must be underway.

Scout the Area Carefully

Thoroughly scout your hunting area and look for scrapes along field edges, creek bottoms, old logging roads, deer trails, open areas in the woods, old homeplaces, *senderos*, and open ridge tops.

When you find scrapes, don't set up on the first ones you find to hunt. Be selective. Make sure the scrapes are fresh. Ask yourself these questions: Is the scrape large, and has it been worked with vigor? Has the dirt been disturbed lately, and is the scrape free of leaves, grass, etc.? Does the dirt have a strong urine odor and/or droppings in or around the scrape? Have the overhanging bushes been chewed or broken and twisted by antlers? Are there fresh rubs in the area?

You want the answers to these questions to be yes. This means you are looking at a scrape that is being worked frequently by a buck. However, don't automatically disregard a smaller, less-used scrape that might simply be new.

I prefer to find three or more fresh scrapes that are close enough together that I can see all of them from my stand and all within range of my bow, handgun, or rifle.

Scout Secretly

Since scouting for scrape hunting is being done at a time when bucks are active at all hours, you must take every precaution to keep your presence a secret. We have all read about how foolish rutting bucks are, and it is sometimes true. But more often than not, if you and several other hunters spook a buck while scouting, he will become very smart very fast and do most of his courting at night.

Be sure to wear cover scent when scouting. Leave as little human odor as possible around rubs and scrapes.

Use caution when moving around in the woods, putting up stands, or talking to fellow hunters. Be as quiet as possible and keep movement to a minimum. Older bucks, thus big-antlered ones, are smart even when rutting and won't put up with much commotion within their territory.

Basic scrape hunting revolves around finding an active scrape.

Sweeten Scrapes

When you have found one or more scrapes that you determine a buck is working regularly, the first step is to determine where you will take your stand, be it a ground blind or portable tree stand. Make sure the wind is blowing from the scrapes to you and that your stand is within range of the scrapes. Also make sure you don't block the buck's logical path to the scrape.

One year at a hunting lodge I was managing, I had a hunter who found a pair of heavily-worked scrapes under the low-hanging limbs of a beech tree. He put up his camouflaged ground blind some 30 yards from the scrapes in the middle of a deer trail leading from a beaver swamp to the edge of the opening where the scrapes were. The hunter hadn't yet gotten settled into his ground blind when he was startled by a grunting sound immediately behind him. He whirled around to stare nose-to-nose at a massive buck in the trail behind his stand. He never saw the buck again.

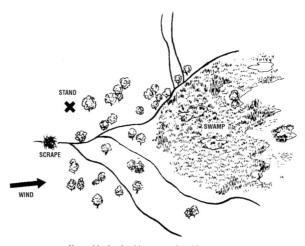

Never block a buck's approach to his scrape.

It's easy to waste time watching false scrapes. Be sure the scrape you are watching is fresh. (Photo by Judd Cooney)

With your blind or stand set up, put a few drops of deer urine in the scrape. Next, use a trick I learned from Francis X. Leuth, a nationally-recognized deer biologist for four decades. Tie a strip of flannel cloth, about six inches long by one inch wide, in the bush overhanging the scrape. Soak the strip of cloth in deer urine. Quickly return to your blind or stand.

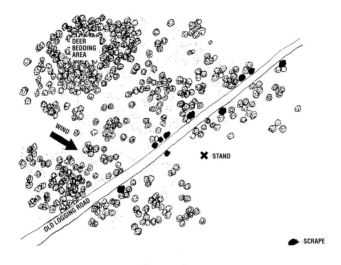

DEER BEDDING AREA

WIND

OLD LOGGING ROAD

✕ STAND

● SCRAPE

Be Alert and Patient

Stay on your stand from before daybreak until dark, and be alert and observant at all times. Serious scrape hunting is hard work. Listen for any unusual sound—excited crows or squirrels, faint grunting sounds, a breaking twig, or slight movement in leaves. Any of these could mean a buck is coming to the scrape.

If at all possible, spend three or more days on a set of fresh scrapes. Sometimes the buck will follow a doe off but return within three days.

On several occasions since I started using the strip of flannel cloth, I have had a buck come to the scrape almost as quickly as I got into my stand. Leuth reasons that the lure scent gets into the air quickly and drifts downwind. If the buck is in that direction, he comes to see if a doe is at his scrape.

Be patient. One reason some hunters have little luck scrape hunting is that they aren't patient. They become bored quickly and move too much, making noise that

Total camouflage, including gloves and a facemask, helps make the scrape hunter more successful.

alerts the buck to their presence. As you sit near a fresh scrape, remember that somewhere nearby is a buck with his ears, eyes, and nose tuned in to detect the presence of a doe in heat. Those same senses can detect you just as well. If they do, you can bet you'll never see him.

Under the right conditions, basic scrape hunting probably offers the deer hunter the best method of taking a trophy whitetail buck. Since scrapes are most often made by bucks that are 2 1/2 years old or older, it is a reasonable assumption that he may have a good rack. It is not uncommon to see a usually-wary buck come to a scrape in the middle of the day using little or no caution, provided the hunter did a good job of leaving no human scent.

Once hunters learn the art of basic scrape hunting and where it will work, it usually becomes an annual event during the season of the rut.

CHAPTER 9

CALLING AT SCRAPES

Deer are vocal animals. Researchers have documented more than a dozen vocalizations, and biologists guess there are many more to be discovered. Of all these sounds, there are two that the scrape hunter should know about, be able to duplicate, and have in his bag of tricks to try on the rutting buck.

Grunt Call

Back in the early 1970's when scrape hunting was finding its way into outdoor magazines, the grunting sound of the rutting buck started getting a lot of attention from readers. Many of them didn't know bucks could make a sound like a low grunt of a hog. Other deer hunters said they had never heard such a sound while deer hunting and questioned if it were so.

The grunting sound has been well documented by deer researchers, and as scrape hunting grew in popularity, call manufacturers were quick to come out with a grunt caller. Reports were being heard of hunters actually using a grunt caller to call bucks to a scrape.

My first attempt at using a grunt caller occurred in Louisiana. For two days, I had hunted three scrapes that were close together on top of a steep ridge. The scrapes were fresh, but hours of sitting in an elevated stand over-

The author used a grunt tube to call this buck to a scrape.

looking them were fruitless. Late the second day, I climbed out of the stand with intentions of scouting the next ridge. I was thinking about changing locations. As I reached the ground, I remembered I had an M. L. Lynch grunt tube in my coat pocket. I decided to blow it a few times, more out of curiosity than anything else.

I gave the tube a few breaths of air, and a series of realis-

Since bucks can pinpoint the location of a caller, total camouflage, cover scent, and remaining motionless are necessary.

tic grunts sounded. In a few minutes, I repeated the process. I waited a few more minutes and decided to put the caller away and walk to the other ridge. As I placed the call into my pocket, I heard something walking in the brush toward me. It stopped about 10 yards away. Only a small thicket of cane was between me and my visitor. As I peered across the head-high cane, I could see the buck's rack, an eight- or perhaps 10-pointer. I couldn't see the brow tines. How I wished I were up in the stand!

I never got a shot at that buck, but it gave me confidence in the grunt call.

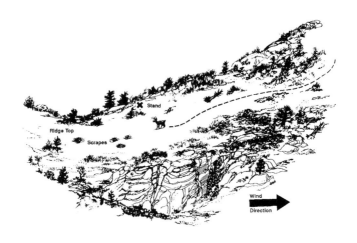

Since then, I have taken several nice bucks by using the grunt call while watching scrapes or in conjunction with rattling. When sitting near scrapes, I use the grunt tube about once every hour. I blow it very softly and in a series of four low grunts. I will do this about once a minute for five minutes. Bucks that come to this call usually sneak in from a downwind position.

Be Inventive

One morning I was watching three fresh scrapes I had sweetened up. At about eight o'clock, I saw a heavy nine-point buck chasing a doe on a far-away ridge. He was followed at a distance by a 10-point buck. It was obvious they weren't coming my way, so I pulled out a Haydel's grunt tube and gave a loud series of grunts. The 10-pointer slid to a halt and looked my way. I gave a series of low grunts. He abandoned the chase and started toward me with his ears laid back. The way he came to me, I wasn't sure if he was

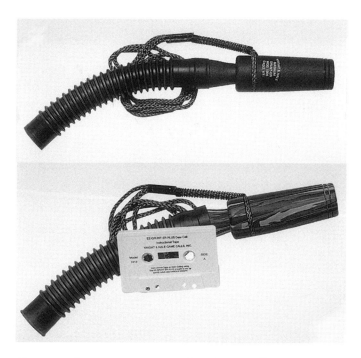

The grunt tube is easy to master and can be very effective during the peak of the rut.

scared but curious or almost ready to fight. Regardless, he is on my wall today.

Rob Keck, executive director of the National Wild Turkey Federation, is not only a renowned turkey hunter, but an excellent deer hunter as well. Keck tells me he has called up some large bucks in South Carolina using the grunt call in a loud, aggressive manner. He blows it a lot more than I would, but it works.

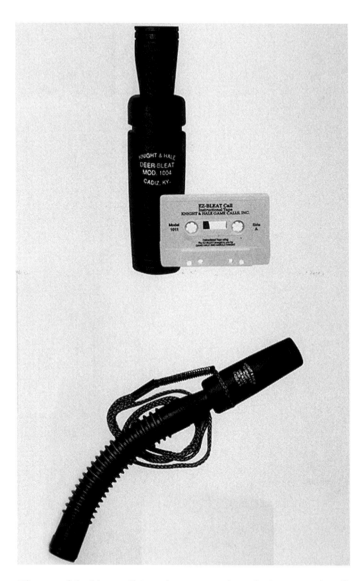

The use of the bleat call is undergoing much study. It can work well near scrapes.

Doe Bleat

A second call that's getting a lot of attention from scrape hunters is the doe bleat. I have little experience with it, but many scrape hunters are reporting success.

The doe bleat is the opposite call of the grunt. Whereas the grunt call is the sound of a buck, the bleat is the seductive call of a doe. It follows the same principles as the hen yelp used during the spring wild turkey mating season. Like the gobbler during mating season, when the buck hears a doe calling during the rut, he is enticed to see if she is ready for love.

Hunters who have used the doe bleat successfully tell me they set up on an active scrape or a close group of scrapes just as though they were basic scrape hunting. They sweeten the scrape with doe scent and take a stand. About once every hour, they will give the sheep-like call of a doe bleat. This is a low call that can barely be heard by a man 50 yards away.

When blowing the caller, hold the bleat for one second. Make five bleats in a series. Wait 10 minutes and do the same thing again. If you see a buck approaching, stop calling and be ready to shoot.

I am told that this is an excellent call to use during the rut to attract a buck that is out in a large field or out of range. The sound of the caller must be kept low, and you must use caution not to overwork this soft, sexy call.

While the grunt and bleat calls may not be necessary to use on every hunt, they are easy to carry. If things are slow, they may be the ticket to making that reluctant buck come to the scrapes you are watching.

Much research is currently being conducted in the field of deer vocalizations. I have no doubt that in the not-too-distant future we will have several new calls to use in deer hunting.

CHAPTER 10

RATTLING AT SCRAPES

In areas with a narrow buck-to-doe ratio, rattling near or at scrapes can be an effective way to call bucks within bow or gun range. When I first started hunting in Texas with hunters who used shed antlers to imitate a buck fight, I couldn't believe it when one or more bucks would come to all that commotion. After taking several bucks rattled in by someone else, I knew I would have to learn this interesting method of calling bucks.

It didn't take me long to learn that there was a lot more to rattling than banging a set of shed antlers together. Rattling, like most hunting methods, requires that you practice the techniques in the right place, at the right time, and under the right circumstances.

Why Bucks Respond to Rattling

Deer managers, deer hunters, and deer call manufacturers have all tried to figure out what attracts bucks to the sounds of two other bucks fighting during the rut. Some say it is the incoming buck wanting to run off the two fighting bucks. Others speculate that the incoming buck is coming to the fight, hoping to steal a doe. There is some research that suggests that bucks are curious and are coming to see what's going on. No one knows for sure. We just have to be glad they do, as it gives us another option for hunting around scrapes.

The urge to check out a fight is sometimes so great that bucks come running in to check out any sound that comes close. Once a friend and I were squirrel hunting with .22 semiautomatic rifles along the banks of the Tombigbee River in Alabama. It was at the same time as the rut. We had a squirrel on the run in the tops of some tall oaks, and both of us were shooting at him. My friend suddenly shouted, "Watch out behind you!" I turned to see a nice eight-point buck slide to a halt, almost touching me. The buck was almost as shocked as I.

Larry Weishuhn once had five mature bucks come in to the sound of a dying javelina's jaw popping. Although he was deer hunting when he shot the javelina, he was quite surprised when the bucks rushed in to the sound. Don't let these unusual stories of bucks coming to rattling-like noises fool you into thinking rattling is easy or that it will work anywhere, anytime during the rut. It's not that way.

Where to Rattle

As with all game calling, rattling will only call a buck if there's one within hearing distance of you. In some open country, that may be 600 to 800 yards, and in some heavily-forested country, it may be only 200 or 500 yards.

A good job of scouting is the best key to successful rattling. Ideally, you need to locate a tract of land with good numbers of bucks and close to equal numbers of bucks and does, say a buck:doe ratio of 1:1 or 1:2. This is important for two reasons. First, there are simply more bucks to hear you and hopefully respond. Secondly, a favorable

Rattling, when used where the buck-to-doe ratio is close, is one of the best scrape hunting techniques for taking large bucks.

buck:doe ratio means that bucks will have to try harder to attract females and are more likely to fight.

This is not to say that occasionally in areas of low buck numbers a buck won't come running in. I have rattled up a few bucks in areas that were over-populated with deer and had low buck numbers. However, the success rate in these cases was very low, and the amount of time spent rattling per buck called in wasn't a good investment.

Rattling should be loud and aggressive when used near the peak of the rut.

Scouting Is Important

Once you have located a tract of land with a narrow buck-to-doe ratio, you must do a good job of scouting. You'll

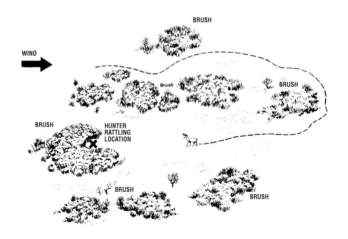

want to find several fresh scrapes located near a bedding area or thick area that provides good cover. Next, you should select an open area from which to call. You can't shoot bucks you can't see. Since a buck may come and go quickly, you need to be set up so you can see around you and get off a fast shot.

If possible, identify several scrape/bedding areas about 500 yards apart. This will give you several rattling locations for use in one day.

Best Time to Rattle

The best time of the rutting period to rattle is during the two weeks prior to the peak of the rut. However, if all else fails, rattling is worth a try at anytime during the entire rutting process.

The best time of the day varies. I have seen bucks rattled up early, late, and at midday. On days following dark nights, early rattling seems to work best. When nights are bright, midday or late afternoon seems to be a good time. On a clear, cold day with no wind, it can be good all day. If the day is windy, select another method of hunting, as rattling doesn't work well in a strong wind. I think that's simply because bucks can't hear the sound.

Proper Set-up

How you set up to rattle can mean the difference between success and failure. While rattling will work from an elevated stand, most hunters prefer to rattle from the ground, as they can add much more realism to the sound.

The site to rattle from should be very near active scrapes. There should be some brush for the hunter to use to break up his outline and to use in making the right sound. The area around the hunter should be thinly wooded or semi-open country. I like to be able to see 50 yards around me, especially downwind.

You may wonder why downwind, as hunters are taught from day one to hunt downwind from our quarry. In this case, you have to think differently. A buck can pinpoint the rattling location as soon as he hears it. He will usually circle that spot until he is downwind from it and then come in. This is especially true of larger, older bucks. The exceptions are usually young bucks.

Since you may be upwind from the deer, you will want to use a cover scent that works well in the area where you hunt. Also, you should wear as much camouflage as the law allows, including facemask and gloves.

As you move to your first set-up and from there to your other previously-selected set-up locations, move as quietly as possible. Walk upwind to the sites, and try to remain

Pick a rattling spot that is downwind from where you expect the buck to come, and be sure your outline is broken up with brush.

unseen. Sneak in. A poor approach can scare off a buck without your ever knowing it.

Finally, once you set up, be sure your bow or gun is within easy reach. As often as not, a buck coming to rattling will run in and leave quickly. Also, some bucks like to sneak in so they're not seen until they are right on you. It is for these reasons that you set up in a fairly open area and keep your gun or bow ready.

The Rattling Sequence

Rattling is successfully done in many different ways by many different people. If you buy a set of rattling "horns" or rattling sticks, follow the manufacturer's instructions to begin with and gradually work in your own additions. If you make your own rattling "horns" from a pair of shed antlers, you may want to follow this sequence, a combina-

Rattling in conjunction with fresh scrapes is an exceedingly deadly hunting technique. (Photo by Judd Cooney)

tion of tricks I learned from rattling masters like outfitter David O'Keeffe, deer biologist Larry Weishuhn, and hunting guide Johnnie Hudman.

If it's early in the rut, bring the antlers together lightly, rattle the tines together several times, and rub some brush. This should not last more than two to three minutes. Repeat every five minutes for 30 minutes. Remember, bucks aren't really fighting hard early in the rut, mostly sparring.

Just prior to the peak of the rut, the fighting between bucks intensifies. The noises made while rattling are loud and aggressive. Begin with a few grunts, then bang the antlers together and push dirt and rocks with your feet. Next, rattle the tines together loudly followed by raking the brush around you with the antlers. This sequence should last from five to 10 minutes. Pause a minute or so and repeat for up to 30 minutes. Remember, you can't be

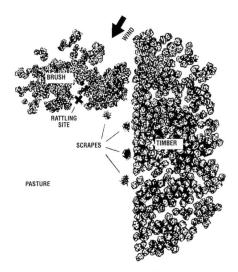

too noisy. Don't be afraid to try different sounds, as no two buck fights are alike.

If nothing shows up for 30 minutes, sit there for another 20 minutes before moving on. Bucks may be circling your position without your knowing it. Once when I was hunting with outfitter David O'Keeffe near Del Rio, Texas, we were rattling at some fresh scrapes that held a lot of promise, but we hadn't seen a buck. O'Keeffe's truck with a high rack on it was parked nearby, and another guide was in the high rack so he could see us in the valley below. The guide watched four nice bucks circle us, but we didn't see any of them.

This brings up another point. If you are trophy hunting, you will want to evaluate the bucks coming in to your rattling. When more than one buck comes in, the first one usually isn't the largest.

Under the right conditions, rattling is a great way to hunt scrapes and a technique every scrape hunter should know.

CHAPTER 11

MAKE YOUR OWN SCRAPES

Not too many years ago, some hunter somewhere reasoned that if you could "freshen up" a buck's scrape and get him to come in to check it, maybe you could get within the home range of a buck and create a scrape of your own. The local buck or bucks would think a bold new neighbor had moved in to claim some of the local girls, and it would get a lot of attention. Whoever this hunter was tried it, and what is now called "mock scrape" hunting was introduced.

Soon after I heard about making mock scrapes, I decided it was worth a try. My first two attempts were such failures, I questioned the merits of mock scrape hunting. I spent four days on each hunt without seeing a buck. My third attempt, however, was a different story. I was hunting a friend's farm in West Virginia. Near his house was an apple orchard that had several scrapes around the edges. For two days I tried basic scrape hunting, but I saw only does, and they paid no attention to the scrapes. However, two of the scrapes were worked by a buck at night.

The third morning, I went into the orchard before daylight. Using a flashlight, I found three likely-looking scrape spots and created three scrapes, complete with limb overhanging each one. To freshen each scrape, I used some fresh urine I had removed from a buck I took the week before in Montana. I even put a drop or two of the urine on the overhanging bush at each scrape.

It is surprising to many hunters that bucks will come to a mock scrape made by a hunter. (Photo by Judd Cooney)

Satisfied with my hastily-made scrapes, I returned to the tripod stand I had erected in the orchard to await daylight. The day spent watching those scrapes was long. Not even a doe showed up to entertain me. Near dark I was thinking about forgetting this make-your-own-scrape business when

I saw a buck squatting on my middle scrape, soaking it with his own stream of urine. He was excited, and so was I.

I saw another occasion that proved man-made scrapes can attract a rutting buck. One year I agreed to teach a bowhunting school at a large hunting club in return for being allowed to stay at the club a few days after the school to hunt. This club had an excellent buck:doe ratio and lots of older age-class bucks.

On Saturday, I taught a course on scrape hunting. To prepare for this, I had gone into the woods near the club's lodge and made five scrapes in a firebreak that had been plowed that fall. When I taught the course, I squirted a little commercial doe urine into each scrape to show how it was done. I also tied a small piece of flannel cloth on the overhanging bush over each scrape and put a drop or two of the scent on it. The course went well and I forgot about it.

The next Tuesday at noon, one of the club members who had arrived the day before came in with a really nice 12-point buck. We all admired it and made pictures of the trophy. At lunch I asked the hunter where and how he had taken the buck. He explained that he found a scrape that morning that was all torn up. It was in a firebreak he was walking in on before daylight. He said he just backed off about 30 yards, found a tree, and put up his portable tree stand. At about 10:30, this buck trotted in to the scrape, grunting. He took it.

"Show me on the map exactly where you were hunting," I prodded him. It turned out to be exactly where I had taught the course.

After lunch he took me to the scrape, and it was one of mine. You should have seen the look on his face when I showed him the cloth strip tied to the overhanging limb. "How do you reckon that got there?" he asked. I never told him the whole story.

Making an artificial scrape is easy. The important part of this hunting technique is to do a good job of scouting and find an area in which a buck or bucks are traveling. You are ahead of the game if you can find some fresh rubs or scrapes as well.

Next, in an area that is logical for a scrape to be located, find an overhanging bush three to six feet above the ground and make a scrape under it. Break off some of the overhanging limbs so it looks like a buck chewed on it. Sprinkle a few drops of buck or doe urine in the scrape and take a stand.

Some mock scrape hunters wear rubber gloves when making the scrape and breaking the overhanging bushes so as to leave no human scent.

Many mock scrape hunters like to make three or more artificial scrapes close together to send out a strong message.

It often takes two to three days for a buck to find the new scrape, but when he does, he checks it out often.

Bill Bynum is one of the most successful mock scrape hunters I know. He shared a unique mock scrape hunting technique with me that can be very valuable when rutting bucks are driven to be nocturnal by heavy hunting pressure.

When bucks are working their scrapes only at night, Bynum breaks out a scrape sweetener he has prepared before the hunting season opens. Here is his recipe:

Place in a clear baby food jar enough small limestone pebbles to almost fill the jar. Limestone pebbles can be purchased at stores that sell aquarium supplies. Next, fill the jar with fresh buck urine. Let it sit tightly closed at least two weeks before using. This lets the urine soak into the pebbles.

With this jar of "sweetener" in his hunting coat pocket,

The buck's nose will often lead him to a man-made scrape.

Rutting bucks tend to cover a lot of ground in search of does in estrus. A well-placed mock scrape should draw their attention! (Photo by Judd Cooney)

With this jar of "sweetener" in his hunting coat pocket, Bynum is ready to take on the nocturnal bucks.

First, he finds an active scrape line. About 10 to 15 yards from an active scrape, Bynum makes an artificial scrape and sprinkles the rank-smelling pebbles into the scrape. Finally, he covers them loosely with soil.

Bynum has found that the bucks will come to this mock scrape during the day and that they will check it out before they will check their own.

CHAPTER 12

DECOYING RUTTING BUCKS

Decoying deer is generally considered to be a new deer hunting technique, and for us modern hunters that may be true; however, early Native Americans' drawings indicate that decoying was one of the earliest deer hunting techniques employed.

Using decoys to attract a rutting buck works well when used around scrapes in some areas. I must admit to some skepticism when I first heard about decoying bucks, but a muzzle-loading hunt in Iowa made me a believer. It had nothing to do with scrape hunting, but it was an educational experience that led to my using decoys with scrapes.

A heavily-used deer trail traced the ridge into a thick bottom, giving the deer good protection from the icy Iowa wind. There wasn't a spot within 35 yards of the trail to place my ground blind without sticking out like a sore thumb. The gusting wind dictated that I not set up the blind near the winding trail. The first day in the blind, I watched deer use the trail out of bow range, fighting the urge to move closer. It was a helpless feeling.

That night back at camp, I noticed a life-size, three-dimensional buck deer target on the bow range and got an idea. I had been reading about the use of deer decoys to attract deer to a specific location and to hold their attention.

Why not use this target as a decoy and make the deer using the trail go where I wanted them to?

Long before daylight the next morning, I placed the decoy right in the middle of the trail, facing the direction the deer had been traveling each morning. My plan was that the deer using the trail would see the buck decoy and move downwind and around it as they studied the strange newcomer. That would put them within bow range of my blind.

I didn't have to wait long after daylight. The first three deer that eased along the trail stopped when they saw the decoy. Slowly they moved off the trail and downwind of the decoy, not taking their eyes off it as they moved to within 10 yards of my stand and stopped. They never knew I was there.

After studying the decoy and testing the wind for any sign of danger, the deer circled back to the trail and went up to the decoy to sniff it. It was fascinating to watch and, needless to say, sold me on the use of decoys.

Why Do Decoys Work?

After I returned home from my Iowa hunt, I set about learning as much as I could about decoying deer. My first move was to talk to an expert on the use of decoys for deer hunting, Dave Berkley of Feather Flex Decoys. Berkley is not only a decoy designer, but also an avid hunter. His company produces life-like waterfowl, wild turkey, and dove decoys. As a student of animal behavior, Berkley reasoned that if other animals could be attracted by the apparent presence of others of their kind, deer could also. He developed a lightweight deer decoy, and sure enough, it worked. But why?

Berkley points out that most of us try all sorts of tactics

Use of decoys is relatively new technology in deer hunting, but is unbelievably effective in conjunction with a variety of techniques. (Photo by Judd Cooney)

This hunter is using a buck decoy in conjunction with a scrape. (Photo by Judd Cooney)

and hunting products, such as calls, scents, camouflage, and other accessories. "The idea is to fool all of the quarry's senses—audio, olfactory, and vision," says Berkley. But if one sense is more trusted and likely to bring an animal in for closer evaluation, it is vision. This is especially true of deer during the rut. Most of us animals depend on our ability to see. Our other senses basically serve to reinforce.

"The true strength of a decoy is in the fact that it demands that the animal focus its sensibilities on an identifiable object, rather than seeking a source which it is unable to see. This makes you, the hunter, less likely to be seen, heard, or smelled," continues Berkley. "We have received numerous reports on the distractive capabilities of decoys. An animal, focused on a decoy, fails to react to a hunter hit-ting his bow on the stand; someone makes a successful draw on a deer while clearly in its field of vision; hunters clearly upwind of alerted animals are successful. Focus of the senses is the key in each case."

Movement Is Key to Attracting Deer

If you want to attract a deer to a specific point, say, to a mock scrape, you can use a decoy to achieve that goal. "For a decoy to be visible to a deer, movement is a key consideration," says Berkley. "The eyes of any animal, including your own, are drawn to movement. The movement doesn't necessarily have to be made by the decoy itself, but by something in close proximity to it. A shaking branch next to the decoy; a fluttering rag or toilet paper; a feather suspended on a string. Anything that will attract attention to the area in which a decoy is located will help deer spot it. Once the decoy is spotted, you now graduate to the next problem."

According to Berkley, the positioning of the decoy is critical—particularly the direction the decoy is facing in relationship to the deer's approach. "The very last thing you want to do is set a decoy 'looking' toward your position," says Berkley. "We find that if a deer sees the decoy while it is apparently being 'seen' by the decoy, face to face, it will approach it in generally a more casual manner than if they see it from the side or the rear."

Berkley contends that a deer approaching from any direction other than head-on will be curious about what an obviously alert cousin is staring at so intently. Approaching deer will generally stare at the same area to see what the decoy is alert to—which is why you never want your decoy facing you.

Berkley recommends tactics that give the decoy an object to "look" at. "The use of our turkey decoys, which have wind-generated movement when placed in the direction

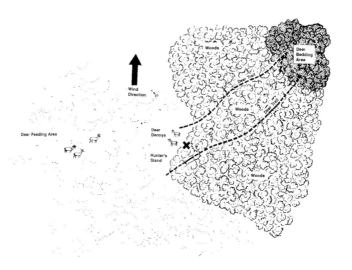

that a deer decoy is 'looking,' seems to give approaching deer an added level of confidence," states Berkley. "We also use two deer decoys 'looking' at each other. One might be set up as a buck and placed on a bush, dead fall, or broken sapling to make it more visible, and the other set as a bedded doe. This particular situation has been further refined by twisting the 'buck's' ears back into an aggressive position. This has been seen to really set a big buck off!"

Berkley has observed that once deer have accepted the decoy as non-threatening, they will interact physically with it—pawing, hooking, or even biting or goring it. "We have yet to see an animal, involved in the above activities, suddenly become aware that it is molesting a fake and run," he said. "The curiosity factor will hold them there until they eventually become bored with it. Left too long in one spot, the decoy will become accepted and ignored. Left overnight, it may be attacked or mauled."

Not every deer is going to be attracted to a decoy, Berkley points out. "I've watched thousands of ducks and

The decoy's "attention" must be focused away from the hunter.

geese fly right past equal numbers of their brothers sitting on the water and never look twice—let alone the number that have flown past my decoy spreads—so enticing and painstakingly set. I've seen deer come around a corner into a green field with four of their brothers peacefully grazing and turn inside out at the sight. The point is that a deer's reaction to a decoy will run the gamut."

Stopping a Buck in His Tracks

We can see from Berkley's experiences how the decoy can be used to attract deer to a specific point, but the decoy can also be employed in other ways.

I have some friends who have worked out a way to use decoys successfully in hunting bucks that spend most of the hunting season in planted pine plantations and won't work their scrapes until night. These dense plantings of pines are thought by most hunters to be unhuntable except around the edges. My friends disagree. They scout out a pine plantation during the stage of the rut when bucks are chasing does until they find a heavily-used trail inside the thick trees. Then they select a point where the trail crosses from one row of trees to another. They will clear out this row middle for 20 to 30 yards and set up an elevated stand.

On the day they hunt the opening, they will position two bedded doe decoys in the opening opposite the stand. The rest is simply waiting for a buck to move into the narrow opening, feeling safe in the thick pine planting. Seeing the does, he will usually stop and stare, giving the hunter plenty of time to get off a shot.

I know a number of hunters who use this technique to get bucks to stop in *senderos* in western states and in power line rights-of-way in several other states.

Pulling a Buck to a Point in a Field

Bowhunters hunting along the edges of large agricultural fields or other openings often spend days observing bucks chasing does, but not within bow range. By using standing deer decoys, such as Flambeau decoys, bucks can be enticed to come within range. It does require some scouting to locate the trails used by deer entering and leaving the field. Locate the standing decoys in the field near these trails and take a stand down-wind.

Sometimes the use of a doe bleat call can be used to at-

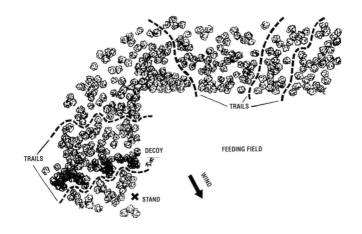

tract attention to these decoys if they are being ignored by deer feeding out in the field.

In open hardwoods during falls when there is a heavy mast crop and does are feeding widely, rather than under a few trees with mast dropping, decoys can be used to pull a buck to one general location. In this situation, it is best to find a stand location where the terrain will help steer the deer to the decoys. One hunter I know finds a place in the woods where two gullies or two beaver swamps come close together. He places his stand and decoys here, and when the buck comes feeding through, it see the decoys. The terrain helps force the buck within eyesight of the decoy.

Another time decoys work well in agricultural fields or in planted food plots is on afternoons during periods of bright nights when deer feed at night and bucks are chasing does at night. Placing two or three decoys out in the field where they can be seen readily by deer in the surrounding woodlands will often coax the deer to come into the field early to feed. I learned this from a wildlife photographer friend who must shoot his photos before dark. During periods of a full moon, he places three or four decoys out in the field in the afternoon; otherwise night-feeding does will come out to the decoys late in the day, and the bucks will follow.

Using Decoys Near Scrapes

Based on my use of decoys and what I have learned from others, the rut can be one of the best times to use decoys. A bedded doe decoy placed near active scrapes and sweetened up with doe urine can get a rutting buck's attention fast. Placing a doe decoy near a stand can give the bowhunter or short-range handgunner an excellent shot.

A standing buck decoy is great to use anytime calling or rattling is practiced near scrapes. The buck coming in to challenge the intruder or the buck that's coming in to see what all the commotion is about is looking for another buck. When he sees the decoy buck, it gives him a point to go to.

One of the most experienced hunters I know who uses decoys has pulled several nice bucks out of thick creekbottoms during the rut using buck decoys. He spends a lot of time patterning bucks prior to the rut. As he locates bucks that are nocturnal and spend their days in thick bottoms, he marks their location on topographical maps. As soon as the rut begins, he places a buck decoy on an open high point near the bottom and sets up his stand. Then, using a grunt tube, he calls to attract the buck. On several occasions he has had bucks run out of the thick cover to challenge his decoy within a few minutes.

When he has trouble calling a buck out of the cover, he will sometimes add a standing doe to the set-up, and it seems to be just enough enticement to lure the dominant buck out of his hiding.

Add Realism to Your Decoy

Like people, deer make eye contact with one another. I have learned that I have much better luck when using decoys with life-like eyes. To do this, I buy glass eyes from my taxidermist and glue them over the eyes of my decoys. They add a touch of reality to my decoys that real deer seem to relate to. When I see the sparkle in the glass eyes, I have more confidence in the decoys.

Keep your decoy free from human scent. I had a friend who stored deer decoys in his tractor shed and got diesel fuel on them. He couldn't understand why they never worked and mine did. Wash your decoys in scent-free detergent and store them in scent-free areas.

Consider using other decoys with your deer decoys to add confidence to the setting. Wild turkeys and crows are always on the alert for danger, so many hunters take along a couple of wild turkey and/or crow decoys to set up near their deer decoys to make incoming bucks feel more at ease.

If you want to add some realistic motion to your deer decoy, glue a triangular piece of white cloth, about eight inches long, to the tail of the decoy. Tie the end of a length of six-pound monofilament fishing line to the point of the white tail and run it to your stand. By pulling on the line you can make the tail twitch like a real deer. This cloth makes a good, absorbent place to add scent to the decoy.

Use Caution When Using Deer Decoys

While decoying deer has proven effective, some states may prohibit the use of decoys. Be sure to check local laws before using decoys.

Be very careful when carrying deer decoys into and out of the woods. Disassemble the decoy before transporting it in the woods. If possible, carry the components in a bright orange bag. Also, wear a bright orange cap and vest when transporting the decoy.

Never place a deer decoy broadside in front of a blind. Position the decoys so your location won't be in the line of fire if shot at by a careless hunter.

Feather Flex decoys are painted so that what is normally white on real deer is bright orange on their decoys. It helps notify other hunters that it is a decoy. I have never known this use of orange on the decoy to scare off a deer. It's a good touch of safety and will probably save lives.

Decoying rutting bucks works. Like other forms of decoying wildlife, it doesn't work every time, and it doesn't always work the way you planned, but it gives us hunters another technique to try while we are enjoying the outdoors.

CHAPTER 13

RUTTING BUCKS TRAVEL THROUGH CORRIDORS

It is pointed out several times in this book that rutting bucks make their scrapes in open areas adjacent to edges. Often a buck will have several scrapes along the edge of a field, others a distance away around an old homeplace, and several more in another part of his territory at the edge of a pasture.

Upon finding several of these scrapes, most hunters will set up a stand where they can see the scrapes and wait for the buck to appear. However, some hunters will ask the question, "How does the buck making these scrapes travel undetected from one line of scrapes to another?" Answer this question and you have an excellent chance of ambushing the buck as he travels.

Study Travel Patterns

I got a real lesson in rutting-buck travel patterns several years ago when I worked on a deer movement study. Our research team had placed radio transmitters on collars around the necks of several whitetail bucks, and we spent many weeks plotting the movement patterns of these deer. One day during the rut I was viewing the maps on which we kept their movements plotted, and an interesting fact jumped out at me. These bucks consistently used narrow corridors that offered heavy cover when moving from one scrape location to another.

A 3½-year-old buck we were monitoring liked to bed down early each morning on a cedar ridge. He would spend several hours there and then get up to look for does. He would move off the ridge to a narrow strip of woods that ran for a half-mile between a paved highway and a clearcut area. At the other end of the woods was a large field newly planted in oats. Here he would work his scrapes. The long, narrow strip of woods was only 50 yards wide and a perfect set-up for a bowhunter.

Another buck would bed down in a swamp on the back side of a cattle farm. During the middle of the day, he would leave the swamp, sneak through a grown-over fence row that was only 15 to 20 yards wide, and enjoy the cattle's salt lick and leftover feed. This buck felt comfortable moving up the corridor created by a grown-over fence row.

Our study showed that bucks will follow a natural fun-

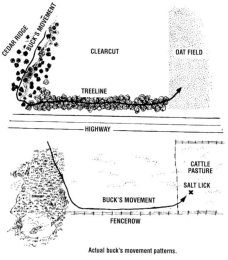

Actual buck's movement patterns.

This trophy buck used a mesquite corridor to travel from his bedding area to his scrape area.

nel if it provides them with cover and leads to an area they want to go to, be it to work scrapes, feed, or bed. Some corridors are geographic in nature. It may be a strip between a creek and the bottom of a steep hill. It could be a long, narrow strip of level land between two deep gullies. It could be a wet, swampy lowland between two fields. In the western states it might be dense vegetation growing along a creek or river running through treeless plains. Many clearcuts have windrows of pushed-up stumps, logs, etc., which form excellent corridors after new growth emerges.

Years ago when I was developing Westervelt Lodge in Alabama, we had two excellent corridors on the property. One was a narrow strip of swampy woods that ran between a busy highway and a large clearcut. The second was a thick band of woods running between a river bank and a busy dirt road. Well-known bowhunter Dan Quillian found both of these highly-productive corridors that linked bedding areas to open areas where the bucks liked to make scrapes.

Don't Overlook the Obvious

Another unusual corridor I discovered was actually in the impact area of the rifle range at another lodge I had in Alabama. The rifle range was built on a large field where we could get shots out to 200 yards. A narrow band of thick woods, actually a grown-up fence row, was the impact area. On the other side of the 30-yard-deep, wooded fence row was a large soybean field. To the south of the range and soybean field was a large swamp, and it was from this swamp that the grown-up fence row ran. Since all shooting was done on the range between the hours of 11 a.m. and 2 p.m., bucks felt comfortable moving up the corridor early and late in the day to work scrapes around each field. One buck that used this corridor would have made the Boone & Crockett record book, but he succumbed to an 18-wheeler one night rather than to some lucky hunter.

I once created a much-used corridor when I cut a large cornfield after the crop had been picked. Running across the center of the field were about a dozen rows of corn I left standing. This gave bucks wanting to cross the field a strip of cover where they could cross without being seen.

One of the heaviest deer trails I've ever seen was in that corridor.

Since these corridors are usually near large open areas or near human activity, most hunters pass by them without ever stopping to scout the narrow areas. Due to this lack of human pressure, rutting bucks feel free to move about these strips.

One such corridor was a narrow strip of thick woods I once discovered running between a sharecropper's house and a large commercial gravel pit area. This strip of woods was almost a mile long. At one end was a national forest boundary, and at the other were some large fields the sharecropper planted in winter wheat each year for temporary pasture. Each day dozens of hunters on their way to hunt in the national forest would ride for almost a mile within 50 yards of this strip of woods. Perhaps it was the sharecropper's 11 kids playing in the yard that kept the hunters away, or perhaps it was the hum and grind of the gravel pit machinery.

While studying a topo map of the area one night, the corridor caught my attention. The next day I met the sharecropper and explained to him I was a bowhunter and would not hunt near his house. He was glad to give me hunting permission and told me the little strip of woods was full of deer every afternoon.

After spending some time scouting, I found his claim not to be exaggerated. Late every afternoon, deer coming out of the national forest would filter along the corridor and feed during the night in the wheat fields. That year I took two nice rutting bucks from the corridor, both within hearing distance of the sharecropper's children playing.

Use a Map for Planning

Not all corridors are deer highways, but to determine which ones are, you need to find several in the area where you hunt to set up for pre-rut scouting trips. One of the best tools to use in locating corridors is a U.S. Geological Survey topographical map, commonly called a topo map, of the area where you hunt. By studying the map, you will see that corridors stand out. Narrow bands of green running across large, open white areas on the map can indicate a corridor. Look for corridors along streams, highways, and railroads. Follow creeks and swamps to see if they go out into fields. Watch the contour lines to see if any natural geographical corridors are formed. Mark all potential corridors so you can obtain permission to scout and possibly hunt the area.

Aerial photographs of your hunting area can show you interesting corridors at a glance. The U.S.D.A. Agricultural Stabilization and Conservation Service office in your county seat has aerial photographs you can review and they can sell you copies if you wish. These photos are like flying over the property in a plane, and corridors stand out when you study the photo.

Scouting corridors should be very thorough. I have known hunters who went into a narrow corridor in only one location and, not finding any deer sign at that spot, abandoned it. Remember, the corridor is usually narrow and long, and that's a lot of area to distribute sign.

Scouting Corridors

I like to scout corridors during the middle of the day when there's plenty of light and less chance of spooking deer. I

Taking a stand in a corridor leading to scrapes can be an effective way to take rutting bucks.

start at one end and zigzag slowly across the strip until I have walked to the opposite end. I look for heavily-used trails, but I'm not discouraged if I don't find them. There may be only one large buck using the corridor, and he won't make a distinct trail. If there is no heavily-used trail, I look for deer tracks and hope for sets of large tracks.

Next, I look for droppings. I like to find droppings scattered throughout the corridor, and I'm especially encouraged when I find droppings that have been on the ground for various lengths of time. This is a good indication that the corridor is used regularly. It has been my experience that you will find the most droppings on the end of the corridor that leads into a scraping or feeding area. Deer, especially older bucks, will often hold up here and wait for dark before venturing into an agricultural field or other opening. This can be a good place to take a stand.

Many corridors, especially those heavily used by does, are sites where bucks choose to make scrapes and rubs. Needless to say, these are good signs to look for during the rut and indicate a great hunting opportunity.

One of the most productive corridors I've ever hunted didn't impress me at all when I scouted it. It was an abandoned road bed running between two large pastures in central Alabama. As I walked through the tunnel-like thicket, I found very few signs such as tracks and droppings. The one thing that did catch my attention was a line of scrapes in the edge of the pasture. On a hunch, I set up a portable tree stand on the side of a pine tree that gave me a good view of the corridor. The second day I sat in the stand, I took a nice 10-pointer at 10:00 in the morning. My friends couldn't believe I took a nice buck out in those pastures.

Hunting Techniques

Determining how to hunt corridors is relatively easy since you are dealing with a somewhat narrow band of terrain in which a buck may travel. If the corridor has a heavily-used trail running through it, it's simply a matter of selecting a stand site near scrapes where the wind will be in your favor. Since corridors may be used only at certain times of the day, I like to determine when they are most likely traveled. An electronic trail monitor can help you answer this question. If you don't want to use one of these, a length of sewing thread tied across the trail about three feet above the ground will give you a good idea if you check it two or three times a day to see when it's broken. If, like many corridors, it is used mainly in the late afternoon, that's when you want to be there.

During the rut, a corridor may be used at any hour, since the buck is constantly in search of a doe in heat. The stand hunter should be alert at all hours during this period. This is a good time to spend the day on the stand.

Since many corridors are extremely thick, it's a good idea to have a portable tree stand on hand. It allows you to look down into the thicket, and if the corridor is narrow, you can see all the way across it. In this situation, it will be hard for a buck to pass by you unnoticed. There are exceptions, however. One year I had found a corridor between a creek and a logging road. This corridor was covered in cane and like a jungle to walk through. I took a portable tree stand and climbed up a water oak high enough to see down into the cane. Once I got into position, I realized I stood out on the side of the tree like a sore thumb, but I decided to put on my camo headnet and gloves and try it anyway.

Just before dark, I could see the cane parting as something moved toward me. I got my bow ready, nocked my arrow, and watched with heart pounding as the cane parted closer and closer. As the cane parted in front of me, I looked down to see a buck crawling through on his knees

Buck corridors can be quite subtle—even a few rows of standing corn in an otherwise open field. (Photo by Judd Cooney)

with his head laid back. I took a shot, but my arrow went over his back. The buck broke into a run and got away. Evidently, he had spotted me and tried to get by me without being seen. I would never have known he was there if I hadn't seen the cane parting.

Many corridors leading to a feeding area where does in heat are feeding can offer two periods of hunting, one late in the afternoon when the buck is on his way in, and early the next morning when he takes the same corridor back to his bedding area. I know a Texas hunter who missed an eight-pointer late one afternoon going through a brushy corridor of mesquite but got him early the next morning when the buck came back through, proof that this concentrated area of travel can pay off.

During periods of heavy snow, corridors can be especially rewarding, as they are often protected from snow and offer easier traveling with some browse thrown in along the way. I have found that corridors sometimes become bedding areas during snowstorms and increase your chances of success.

Corridors offer the scrape hunter an alternative to sitting on scrapes and, in heavily hunted areas, may be the best place to hunt.

CHAPTER 14

HUNTING THE RUT
WITHOUT SITTING
ON A SCRAPE

Several years ago, I had what was not a typical deer hunting season for me. I usually spend several days during the rut hunting scrapes for big bucks, but that year my hunting lodges were full and demanded most of my time. As the rut reached a peak, I only had a few hours I could devote to hunting. There just wasn't time to scout for scrapes and watch them from a stand for several days. A new tactic was needed.

During the weeks prior to the rut, several hunters had told me about seeing a large number of does and yearlings at a certain creek crossing on the lodge property. Since I knew that bucks in rut travel almost constantly looking for does in heat, I felt the creek crossing might be a good place to spend an hour or so I had available for hunting. This would have to take the place of scrape hunting.

It was well after daylight when I sat down at the base of a large red oak tree. My stand gave me a good view of a well-used deer trail which came down the steep banks of the creek at a point where the creek was very shallow. The shot would be only 80 yards from my sitting position; I felt confident that if a buck used the crossing, it would be an easy shot.

I had hardly gotten settled when the first of several does slid down one bank, crossed the creek, and climbed up the other bank. Within 20 minutes, 11 does and yearlings had made their way across the misty creek. Each time, I felt sure a buck would follow, but none did.

It was getting late, and I needed to get back to the lodge. As I started to get up from my comfortable stand, a doe slid down the embankment and stopped in the creek to watch her backtrail. With her tail held high, she climbed the other bank. At the same time, a nice six-pointer slid down the bank and entered the creek, following close behind the doe. I placed the crosshairs of my scope on his front shoulder and touched off the .243. Just as the buck fell, I saw two more bucks, much larger-racked than the one I had just shot, run back down the trail the six-pointer had just come down. If I had waited just 30 seconds more! All three bucks were following the last doe, and the creek crossing was just as good a stand as a line of scrapes.

There are several tactics other than scrape hunting that can be used to take rutting bucks, but first one must understand a few things about a buck's habits during the rut.

A buck doesn't collect a harem of does. However, he may be seen in the company of several does. During the rut, he will service a doe and leave looking for another doe in heat.

During this period, the buck eats very little and travels with a doe in heat or nearing the heat period, or he travels looking for a doe that may be coming into heat.

A hunter may encounter a buck at any time during the rut, especially if does are present. Bucks are doing a lot of moving around at that time, often carelessly.

One of the best tactics to use during the rut is a combination of stalk hunting and stand hunting. The idea is to increase the chances of buck encounters by covering a number of likely areas in one day. Always remember that during the rut, a buck may appear at any time.

With notes taken from pre-season scouting, the hunter can plan his stalk/stand tactic before the hunt takes place. I like to use an old logging road as the base for my stalk/stand hunt. The road is open and usually quieter to walk in. I will ease along the road for some 10 minutes, and then move off the road to sit for 30 minutes to one hour, watching an oak grove, a beaver swamp, a deer trail, or any other feature that scouting has told me deer might be using. After a session of sitting, I once again get back into the road and ease along to my next stand. A friend of mine likes this method of hunting, but prefers to stalk along the base of a ridge rather than in a logging road.

For this method of hunting to be successful, one must keep the wind in his favor and move very slowly. Each sound must be evaluated, as deer make many sounds which can give the hunter early warning that deer are near. The hunter must look carefully and be aware of parts of

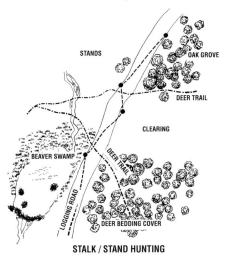

STALK / STAND HUNTING

deer. Often all you will first see is the shine of an eye, the horizontal line of the back, the point of an ear, the white of an antler, or the twitch of the tail. Binoculars are an important tool to use when stalk/stand hunting.

Sit perfectly still with your back to a tree to break up your outline. If you like to stand up, lean against a tree. Blend in with your surroundings.

A second method of hunting during the rut is to locate areas where does are feeding. This may be a creekbottom covered in greenbrier, food plots planted in wheat, oats, or rye, agricultural crops, or oaks during years of good mast production. Wherever does are found during the rut, you will find bucks. Selecting a good stand overlooking these feeding areas gives the hunter a chance to see a buck moving among the does. In areas where does are feeding on agricultural crops, I like to use a ladder-type stand and get into small patches of woods growing between fields. Often it is within these same patches of woods that deer move to reach a field. (Be sure to read the chapter on hunting corridors.)

On food plots, I like to locate a stand back into the woods some 20 to 60 yards to observe deer before they move out into the opening. I have often seen bucks stand around in the woods watching a food plot for long periods of time before actually going out into it.

A portable treestand is valuable if you are going to hunt thick feeding areas such as greenbrier or honeysuckle.

Hunting feeding areas being used by high numbers of does is usually better late in the afternoon, but anytime the does are out there, be observant for bucks as well.

Since bucks are moving a great deal during the rut, stands located near well-used deer trails are often very productive. The creek crossing I mentioned earlier in this chapter was a classic example of how a trail heavily used by

Using a canoe to locate overlooked rutting bucks can be another way of hunting during the rut.

does paid off. You may even find a spot where several trails come together, such as at a choice feeding area, a low saddle between two steep ridges, or at an easy crossing on a stream. If you find such a location and there is evidence such as fresh droppings, fresh tracks, or fresh slides where the deer have slid down a stream bank, you have found an excellent location for a stand where there is a concentration of deer movement.

A portable tree stand lets the scrape hunter be as flexible as necessary to outsmart a rutting buck. (Photo by Judd Cooney)

The rut means buck movement, which is often unpredictable. Hunters need to use their imagination to waylay a trophy. (Photo by Judd Cooney)

If you see a doe, become alert, as she is likely to be followed by a buck. He may be moving much more cautiously as much as 30 minutes behind her, although during the rut he may be less wary than usual. When you do see a buck moving into range, take your time in mounting your rifle. Make your moves when he has his head down or is looking the other way. Remember, take your time and pick your shot.

If you elect to stand hunt for moving bucks during the rut, follow these tips:

• Use a quality binocular. I prefer a 7x42 roof prism, armor-coated binocular. By watching the areas farthest from my stand, I often see deer moving my way long before they get into range.

• Determine wind direction, even when there appears to be no wind at all, so you can hunt downwind from deer.

• Wear yellow shooting glasses when hunting in dark timber, when stalk hunting, and while hunting during periods of low light, as they enable you to see much more clearly. They are also an aid in scouting for whitetail deer, allowing the hunter to better detect signs and deer movement.

• Keep muscles loose. Sitting still in a tree stand or in a ground blind can cause your muscles to tighten up. I always make it a practice, when in a blind or stand, to take a few moments each hour to stretch, move my arms, move my legs, draw my bow, or point my rifle to flex my muscles. The sacrifice of a few moments of movement is worthwhile, as when that moment comes to draw your bow or shoulder your rifle, you can do so much more easily.

• Wear headnet and gloves. I have learned from turkey hunting that by using a camouflage headnet and cotton camouflage gloves, I see many more deer than I did in the past. Not only do these items help camouflage the hunter, but I have found that a headnet helps keep my face and head much warmer by trapping warm air inside it.

If you are one of those hunters who can't sit still for long periods of time, the rut is one of the best times of the season for stalk hunting. During this restless period, I've seen bucks in the middle of the day walking down the same logging road I was sneaking down. I've seen them boldly walk across the middle of an open field. The stalk hunter may see a buck anywhere, and for those who can move painstakingly slowly and remain constantly alert, the stalk hunt can be an excellent method of hunting during the rut.

The rule for the non-scrape hunter during the rut is to capitalize on the restlessness of the breeding buck. Use methods that will give you the best chance to catch him moving around or those that will put you near his goal—the breeding doe. By doing this, you will encounter a buck in pursuit of a mate.

CHAPTER 15

ARMED FOR SCRAPE HUNTING

Scrape hunting, whether you are sitting on a scrape, rattling or calling near a scrape, or ambushing bucks on their way to a scrape, is ideal for bowhunters, handgun hunters, and blackpowder hunters. Most shots are at close range, often 10 to 20 yards. This was one of the reasons I became a student of scrape hunting back in the 1960's. I was an avid bowhunter and was looking for hunting techniques that would put bucks within 25 yards. Scrape hunting offers that in most of its forms.

Muzzleloaders

A few years later I became interested in hunting whitetails with muzzleloading rifles, some of which were accurate to only 75 yards. Once again, I found scrape hunting to be the best way to score on bucks within my effective range. Even today, with accurate, 125-yard-range muzzleloaders such as the CVA Apollo, Modern Muzzle Loading MK-85, and the Thompson/Center Thunderhawk and Scout Carbine, I still prefer to do much of my muzzleloader hunting during the rut to improve my chances of getting a shot at a buck within range.

Since most shots taken while scrape hunting are under 100 yards, short-range brush rifles are ideal for the scrape hunter.

Handguns

For several years now, I have enjoyed handgun hunting whitetails with both short-range calibers such as the .41 Magnum, .44 Magnum, or .454 Casull, as well as longer-range calibers like the 6.5 JDJ and the .35 Remington. Scrape hunting offers the short-range handgunner who is limited to whitetails within 100 yards or less the same chance at a trophy buck as a rifle hunter. The advantage to handgun hunting, other than the interesting challenge it

One of the author's favorite scrape hunting rifles is the Ruger No. 1 International in 7x57mm.

provides, is that it offers the convenience of having the hands free to climb stands or rocks, push through brush, or simply move freely.

Shotguns

Now more than ever before, deer hunters are being required to use slug-firing shotguns for deer hunting in densely populated areas. Both the modern slug gun and slug loads have been developed to a degree of accuracy unknown in the past. Some slug shotguns, equipped with rifled barrels and shotgun scopes and firing sabot slugs, can shoot a two-inch group at 125 or so yards. These accurate, short-range guns are becoming more popular with scrape hunters, even those who hunt where slug guns are not required.

Rifles

If you really want to start a heated debate around the campfire, get a group of scrape hunters started discussing the question of what is the best rifle for the serious scrape hunter. While everyone seems to have a different idea on the subject, there is a trend toward short-range rifles with carbine-length barrels, and I agree with this choice. These compact rifles are easy to carry through brush, while climbing rocks, and while getting into and out of elevated stands. In the right calibers, they are sledgehammers at 150 yards, the range within which most bucks are taken by scrape hunters.

These guns are often referred to as "brush guns," not because their round-nose bullets will plow through brush and stay on course—no bullet will do that—but because the short rifles are ideal for carrying through thick brush and are fast to get into shooting position. Among the favorites of scrape hunters are such lever-action rifles as the Marlin Model 336 in .30-30 Winchester or .35 Remington, Marlin Model 1895 in .45-70 Government, and Winchester Model 94 in .30-30 Winchester, .307 Winchester or .356 Winchester.

Single-shot fans will like the Ruger No. 1 International in 7x57mm, Ruger No. 1 Medium Sporter in .45-70 Government, New England Firearms Handi-Rifle in .30-30 Winchester, and the Thompson/Center Contender Carbine in 7-30 Waters or .375 Winchester.

A compact, bolt-action rifle that has won favor among many scrape hunters is the Remington Model Seven in 7mm-08 Rem.

This is not to say that the dozens of popular bolt-action, semiautomatic, and single-shot models in long-range calibers are not equally good; they are. But hunters who want

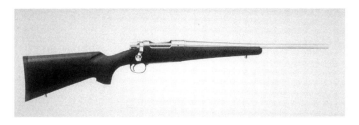

Perhaps the most popular rifle used by scrape hunters is the Remington Model Seven.

The New England Firearms Handi-Rifle is a compact single-shot rifle many scrape hunters use.

A long-time favorite rifle for scrape hunting is the Marlin Model 336.

to use shorter-range arms and calibers must be more selective in their hunting methods and terrain, and scrape hunting can offer their best opportunity to use these arms.

One additional benefit that has come from this renewed interest in brush guns by scrape hunters is that many of these compact rifles are ideal for young or small-framed hunters. When equipped with a rifle that fits, a hunter can shoot better. The beginning hunter who scrape hunts stands a chance of taking a good buck sooner.

Scrape hunting, for the most part, is short-range hunting. It offers opportunities for the hunter with short-range equipment to have the hunt of a lifetime.

The exact rifle, handgun, bow, or shotgun isn't nearly as critical in scrape hunting as the hunter's ability to use it quickly and accurately! (Photo by Judd Cooney)

CHAPTER 16

PUTTING SCRAPE HUNTING TO WORK

You now have all the ingredients that go into scrape hunting. But reading about it is just the first step. Now you have to take the information in this book and apply it to your own hunting situations.

In some cases, you may have to hunt a corridor or sit on a secluded creek crossing because the local hunting pressure has the rutting bucks working scrapes only after sundown. Other situations may have you calling bucks to scrapes or rattling in rutting bucks. Or, it may be as easy as finding some freshly-worked scrapes and sitting in a blind watching them. That decision-making process can only be gained from experience and knowledge of your hunting area; after all, that is a vital part of the hunting adventure.

One of my favorite hunting adventures was a handgun hunt that would have been unproductive had I not been an experienced scrape hunter. Consider my decision-making process and the scrape-hunting principles applied as you read about it.

I was hunting in a narrow valley through which Chitlin Creek flowed. It was an area not known for producing trophy bucks. In fact, the area didn't have a large deer population, and few hunters ever ventured into the jungle-like tangle of small trees, vines, and brush covering the valley and surrounding slopes.

The honeysuckle offered the buck plenty of food, the thick vegetation gave him cover, water was plentiful, and no one ever hunted in the little valley. What a perfect hideaway for a buck. I would return.

I knew the area around the Chitlin Creek homestead would be ideal for handgun hunting. The thick cover made long shots impossible, and it made traveling or stalking with a long-barreled gun a difficult chore.

After much consideration, I elected to hunt there with my Remington XP-100 bolt-action, single-shot handgun. It's a favorite brush gun of mine due to its short, 14½-inch barrel and light weight; with a scope, it weighs only a little over five pounds. Its nylon stock is virtually indestructible, so I knew it could take the abuse of crawling through thick brush.

Another reason I chose my XP-100 is that it is chambered in .35 Remington. Firing Remington 200-grain soft point Core-Lokt ammunition, this caliber is a sledgehammer on big whitetail bucks at ranges out to 150 yards.

To be equipped for any range shot the Chitlin Creek hunt might present, I mounted a Simmons 2.5-7x28 handgun scope on the XP-100 using a Burris mounting system.

The handgun, scope, and load combination proved to be an accurate team on the range. From a sandbag rest at 100 yards, the 200-grain load printed 1½ to two-inch groups. Not only did I practice from the bench, but I spent several afternoons practicing with the handgun in field positions, such as bracing on the side of a small tree. I didn't want poor marksmanship to keep me from taking the buck.

Many evenings that fall were spent studying topographical maps and aerial photographs of the Chitlin Creek area. I got to know the terrain as best one can with a limited

When you put it all together, scrape hunting techniques can lead you to many outstanding hunting adventures.

amount of time on the property. I wanted to be ready when opening morning rolled around.

Long before daylight on the first day of the whitetail season, I groped my way to a hillside that rose behind the homestead site. I found an opening on the slope and sat down to await dawn.

As the pink fingers of light in the east gave way to a rising sun, I realized I could see no more than 20 yards in any direction. I wasn't sure I could find a spot with more visibility in the thick tangle without making too much noise, so I stayed on the cold slope for most of the morning. All I saw were two gray squirrels playing in a distant red oak.

By midday I had concluded that I must get to know the area much better; just sitting in the woods was not the way to hunt this buck. I spent most of the afternoon scouting the area slowly and quietly. There was little sign to be found, but I did see old rubs on small trees near the old homesite. Along the creek, true to the angler's word, I

The "flehmen behavior" is typical of the rut; the buck is literally "tasting" scent molecules. (Photo by Judd Cooney)

found deer tracks, but only on gravel bars. These were difficult tracks to locate. It was almost as though the buck knew that someone would be trying to track him.

Late that evening, I took a stand on one of the creek crossings. On a slight rise overlooking the crossing grew a thick stand of wild plum and gum saplings. I backed into those bushes and sat where I could see the creek crossing and the approach from both sides.

As the sun slipped below the western horizon, the air in the damp valley grew colder. My hopes began to fade. Suddenly I spotted a movement to the left of the stream. I eased the XP-100 up on my knee and into a ready position. A doe eased out and slowly, cautiously waded the creek. I was enjoying watching her when I saw a second deer emerge along the same route. There stood the Ghost Buck. My heart raced as I watched the buck looking at the doe that was disappearing into the brush on the opposite side of the creek.

I took my eyes off the buck just long enough to spot the gum sapling that I was easing the handgun up to for a shooting rest. When I moved my eyes back to where the buck had stood, he was gone. Without a sound. No wonder the old man considered him a Ghost Buck.

The next morning I returned to the same stand in the sapling thicket, but my only reward was to watch a red fox pass by with a cottontail rabbit in its mouth.

At noon I walked back to the old homestead site to explore its remains and eat my lunch. As I was sitting next to the chimney thinking what a peaceful place this must have been to live, I was curious about where the barn might have been located. It had to be nearby. I began to walk around the house site in ever-widening circles, and down the little valley some 150 yards from the chimney, I found the remains of an old fence. There, on a fence post, hung the metal rim of a wagon wheel. I pushed my way through a thick growth of honeysuckle and poplar saplings to find a somewhat open area that was thinly forested in old apple

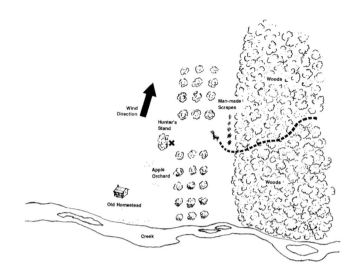

and pear trees. I had stumbled upon the homestead orchard. Several small pine trees grew among the fruit trees,
and some of the pines were freshly rubbed. I felt a rush of
excitement.

Further scouting around the old orchard revealed five
large scrapes along the edge of the opening. Each scrape
was freshly pawed with a recently broken limb hanging
over it. I had found the Ghost Buck's honeymoon suite.
Now to decide how to hunt it.

The orchard was at least two acres in size. When I tried
several ground blind sites, my vision was blocked by low-
growing vegetation. I needed to be in an elevated blind.
Several large oaks grew around the edges, a couple in great
locations to see all five of the scrapes, but none with low-
growing limbs that I could climb.

Back in camp in my truck was a portable ladder stand
called "The Griz," made by Trax America. I could mount
the 10-foot ladder stand and see the entire opening.

A fresh scrape properly utilized is one of the best opportunities a hunter can have for that one shot at a fine buck! (Photo by Judd Cooney)

The remainder of the day was spent walking back to camp and packing the stand back into the old orchard at Chitlin Creek. By the time I had the stand in place, it was dark.

Two hours before daylight the next morning, I was on my way to the stand. It was the expectation of a successful hunt that carried me through the thick brush in the darkness of that cold, pre-dawn morning.

As the first light appeared, I checked out the padded guard rail on the stand. It made a perfect rest for the XP-100, and I could get a clear shot at many areas in the old orchard. Most importantly, I would be able to see all five scrapes.

With the growing light came a fog that gave the opening an unearthly appearance. I hoped the fog would burn off quickly. Within an hour it abruptly disappeared, and there, to my surprise, lay a doe near one of the scrapes. She seemed to be waiting for the Ghost Buck to appear. Occasionally she would look around as though expecting company at any time.

The morning advanced and no buck appeared. I became concerned that in my haste to put up a stand, I may have unknowingly scared the buck. As I sat in the stand thinking of what all could have gone wrong, I heard a faint grunt off at a distance. I couldn't tell which direction the sound came from. The doe heard it, too, and she looked into the thick woods behind her. Then came two loud grunts. At this, the doe jumped up and ran across the old orchard, passing almost directly under my stand. I sat the XP-100 on the padded guard rail and watched the woods line near where the doe had been lying.

Without a sound, the buck emerged, his nose in the air and his lips curled back. I pushed the safety off and found the buck's shoulder in the scope. As he turned back toward the thick cover, I squeezed the trigger. The handgun jumped in my hand, and I heard the bullet hit home. The Ghost Buck went down.

It took me three hours to get the buck to a point where I could get my truck to it. As I loaded the nice eight-pointer, the old fisherman walked up with his short cane pole on his shoulder.

"I see ye got him, Sonny," he grinned. "Thought ye might."

He paused, then continued. "Did I tell ye about the big 10-pointer I've been seeing a little futher down the creek at the ol' Taylor place? He's sort of a Ghost Buck, too."

"Let's sit down and talk," I said to my friend. He had my attention.

It's hunting like this that makes scrape hunting one of the whitetail hunter's most valuable skills. No two hunts will be alike, but if you find scrapes, you know you have a buck to hunt and the skill to do it right.

INDEX

Note: Bold page numbers indicate illustrations or photos.

WHITETAIL SECRETS
VOLUME THREE — SCRAPE HUNTING FROM A TO Z

Color photography by Charles J. Alsheimer
Pages 4, 14, 24, 78, 88

Color photography by J. Wayne Fears
Pages 32, 40, 56, 68, 96, 106, 128, 140, 150, 158

Color photography by Judd Cooney
Page 114

Illustrated by David Baer

Designed by Kirby J. Kiskadden

Text composed in Berkeley by
E. T. Lowe Publishing Co.
Nashville, Tennessee

Color Separations and Film prepared by
Kirby J. Kiskadden

Printed and Bound by
Quebecor Printing, Kingsport, Tennessee

Text sheets are acid-free Warren Flo Book by
S. D. Warren Company

Endleaves are Rainbow Parchment by
Ecological Fibers, Inc.

Cover material is Taratan II Bonded Leather
by Cromwell

A handsome man fell in her spell.
The way into her chamber straightaway he took.

PHARISEE 1: Why wait we then. Quick! Let's test
   this fact,
   And gaze upon this sinning beauty,
   And catch them in this shameful act,
   Only, of course, as it is our duty.

LUCIFER: By law she should be stoned to death
   For dire adultery.
   Bring her we before Jesus in his sight,
   Try then to tempt him if we might,
   And test whether he will judge her right
   Or else unlawfully.
   If he bid her punished sore,
   He goes against his own lore
   That he hath preached here before:
   Merciful men should be.

PHARISEE 1: If he hold to his idle parlance,
   And preach of mercy her for to save,
   Then we have matter of much substance
   Him for to kill and put in his grave.

PHARISEE 2: Good counsel this all be.
   Set there thy shoulder with all thy might.
   Break up the door and in our sight
   Her trespass shall herself indict.

*(They break down the door. A young man runs out in
his doublet, his boots untied and holding his breeches in
his hand.)*

PHARISEE 1: May Great God's curse go with thee,
   That you do meddle with a whore.

YOUNG MAN: That same curse I give you three,
   And wish you all in hell full sore.

(Lucifer laughs)

21

YOUNG MAN: *(to the audience)* In faith I was so sore afraid
  Of yon three shrews, the truth to say
  I could not get my breeches on,
  I had so fast to run away.
  I am full glad that I am gone,
  And God's curse have ye, everyone.

PHARISEE 1: Come forth thou wanton, come thou whore,
  Come forth thou sloven, come forth thou slut.

PHARISEE 2: We shall teach thee with torment sore
  To foul our city with your smut.

PHARISEE 1: Come forth slattern, come forth thou filth,
  Come forth thou bitch and brothel bold.

(the woman is dragged forth)

WOMAN: *(as they go off)* A mercy, mercy, sirs I you pray.
  For all my sins I'm sore to blame.
  I pray you slay me now, here this day.
  Let not the people learn of my shame.

(They go off. Jesus and his party enter. The two Pharisees enter, leading the woman taken in adultery. Lucifer hovers unseen in the background.)

JESUS: *(preaching)* Nolo mortem peccatoris.
  No death for sinners. I say you this:
  If man, for his sin take repentance;
  If he amend that is amiss,
  Then heaven shall be his inheritance.

PHARISEE 1: Hark, sir prophet, pious we pray
  You, give true doom and dire sentence
  Upon this woman, which this same day
  In sinful adultery has done offense.

(the second Pharisee catches sight of Lucifer, who nods encouragingly)

PHARISEE 2: Moses law bids us stone
All such as be unclean.
So we bring her here to you alone
For judgment to be seen.

(Jesus writes in the earth)

JESUS: Now which of you, either one,
  is without sin? Tell him anon
To cast the first stone.
Believe it, or be gone.

PHARISEE 2: What writest thou master?

(he looks at the writing)

PHARISEE 2: Out alas, much woe is me!
For no longer dare I here be,
For dread of worldly shame.

(he flees)

PHARISEE 1: Why now, fellow, why does thou flee?

(he looks at the writing, then flees)

I will go to him and see.
Away now must I also dance,
At least as far as France.

JESUS: Now wrote I in clay for them to see
Their own sins. I knew them to be.
And each one then did fearful flee,
They fled at but the glance.

(Lucifer leaves in disgust)

WOMAN: Oh holy prophet, mercy I plea.
With all my heart I am sorry.

JESUS: I do not thee condemn. Repent.

Of all thy deeds I make thee free.
Let thee no more to sin assent.

WOMAN: Lord, most blessed must thou be,
That from misdeed has helped me.
Henceforth filth I will flee
And thee follow in good faith.

(the other disciples enter)

JESUS: Now go we to Jerusalem's gate.
Friends await me, and my fate.

(song)

(A session of Jewish magistrates: Annas, Caiphas, and attendants. Roman soldiers guard. Barabbas stands in the dock.)

BAILIFF: Judge Caiphas, this man, Barabbas, a thief of renown,
Has been found with his hand in another's purse.

ANNAS: As ill might the feet be that brought thee to town.
Barabbas, thou thief, receive thou my curse.
Bring him to the Romans. There thorns be his crown.
Who steals from his fellows can do no worse.

(the soldiers drag Barabbas away)

CAIPHAS: Now, Annas, what of this Jesus, whom you would condemn?

ANNAS: Judge Caiphas, as prelate it is my duty to preserve the peace,
Consequently, I must enforce the law.
This Christ must now in full his false claims cease.
This traitor must his blasphemy withdraw.

24

CAIPHAS: We who are by our Roman rulers named,
Cannot in haste against this Christ proceed.
If treason is indeed 'gainst him proclaimed,
Such charges grave, to death must certain lead.

ANNAS: Know you, Christ continues the people to
blind.
Claims he is king of Jews and all mankind.
Treason this is, I say to thee,
For Caesar is king and none but he.

ADVISER: And sir, remember the great charge that
on you is laid
To keep the law. For should you fail,
Our Roman lords must for that be paid;
We Jews, in truth, will they assail.

CAIPHAS: Now, brethren, then will you hear my
intent?
These nine days let us abide.
We may not give so hasty judgment.
Now send you spies the country wide,
To see and record as testimony.
And then his works he cannot hide
Nor have the power them to deny.

ANNAS: I will accept this judgment.

*(A busy street. Lucifer enters. He has a hand micro-
phone. Lucifer addresses the audience. He is gorgeously
dressed like a young gallant. His tone is boastful and
hectoring.)*

LUCIFER: I am your lord, Lucifer that out of hell
came,
Prince of this world, great duke to you each.
Wherefore to you, Sir Satan, my name—
Who appeareth here a point pressing to preach.
Once I was sustainer of sin, the entrapper of
men,

Dragged to my deep dungeon there doomed to remain.
So great did I reward him then
He did ever sing wellaway in piteous pain.

But, so bounteous a lord changed am I,
To now reward sinners. Am I not kind?
Who so will follow my lore and serve me thereby,
Of sorrow and pain enough he never shall find.

Give me your love, grant to me affection
And I will disclose the treasure of that love's alliance,
Grant your desires, according to your intention.
No poverty shall approach you, just plentiful abundance.

Behold the diversity of my fancy attire,
Each part in its place, the effect so harmonious,
Appearing exactly as its function require,
From the sole of my foot to my head ceremonious.

(The crowd cheers. John the Baptist, also with a hand mike, addresses the audience. He and Lucifer are not unlike political candidates vying for the attention of the electorate. In the crowd are spies for Caiphas and Annas.)

JOHN: I, John Baptist, to you thus prophesy;
That one shall come after me and not tarry long,
One many fold more stronger than I.
Wherefore I counsel thee ye reform all wrong.
Hold your conscience of the deadly sins, seven,
And for them do penance, speed from sin strong,
For now shall come the kingdom of heaven.

LUCIFER: Blind beggars and poor people, you should them despise.
Swearing and lechery will bring you delight.

To maintain thy position to bribe be but wise.
And if the law reproach thee, say then thou wilt
  fight.

JOHN: The path that lies to this blessed inheritance
Is hope and dread coupled by conjunction.
Betwixt this prime pair may be no severance,
For hope without dread is manner of
  presumption,
And dread without hope is manner of
  desperation.

LUCIFER: Pay heed to no precept, or no one's
  commandment,
Not civil nor clerical, set them aside
Let mention of God be met with oaths repugnant.
For sin is not shameful, nor boldness and pride;
And your reward, you shall in hell abide.

JOHN: Sin not in the hope that sin be made clean
By merciful God who makes all repair;
But if by sensuality as is often seen
Thou weaken, thou shalt not therefore despair.
Therefore do penance and confess thy sin.

*(Christ is led through the streets of Jerusalem by his
disciples)*

JOHN: *(preaching)* O ye people despairing, take heart!
A great cause ye can have. Ye can see
The Lord that from whom all things start.
He's coming your comfort to be.

BLIND MAN: Lord, mine eyesight from me is hid;
Grant it to me. I cry mercy.
This would I have.

JESUS: Look up now with cheer blithely.
Thy faith can save.

BLIND MAN: Thou, king of bliss, loved may ye be,

That thus my sight has sent me soon,
And by great skill.
I was as blind as any stone;
I see at will.

JESUS: As I love this man so you shall
And all of you so, to each other.
Humble of heart we are all equal:
Each of us is the other's brother.

Live thy lives in charity
And in heaven shall I reward thee.

(Caiphas's and Annas's spies confer. Jesus speaks to the lame man.)

JESUS: Man rise; cast thy crutches forth from thee.
You need them not.
And look in truth thou steadfast be
And follow me forth with good intent.

LAME MAN: Lord, lo my crutches, where they flee
Upon this spot.
Such grace has thou showed unto me
As thou art from heaven sent.

(Jesus is met by a crowd, many carrying palm branches. Again the spies are there.)

JESUS: Friends, behold the time of mercy
The which is come now, without any doubt.
Man's souls in bliss now are sanctified
But the prince of the world is cast out.

CITIZEN: Hail, prophet proven, without a peer!

ALL: Hail!

CITIZEN: Hail, Prince of Peace, the price thou paid.

ALL: Hail!

CITIZEN: Hail, king comely, courteous, and clear.

ALL: Hail!

CITIZEN: Hail, flourishing flower that ne'er shall
    fade.

ALL: Hail!

CITIZEN: Our brother Moses said thereby
    A new prophet shall God restore.

ALL: Hail! Our king is he.

(Lucifer on the scene)

DEVIL 1: The people, by his works and words are
    greatly impressed.

DEVIL 2: And crowds throng thickly by him to be
    blessed.

DEVIL 1: Thou, Satan, must this dastard drag down
    to his doom.

DEVIL 2: Or hell he will cast in perpetual gloom.

LUCIFER: Now shall his truth be tried and no
    further his heresy.
Now his soul from his body shall make separation.
Now the time draweth near of his persecution.
I shall devise new charges of malicious conspiracy.
Plenty of reproofs I shall provide to his
    confusion,
And falsify the words that his people doth testify.
His disciples shall forsake him and his mastery
    deny.
Innumerable his wounds that shall all men horrify.
A traitor shall him betray, his death to fortify.
The rebukes that he gave me shall he himself
    damnify.

*(An anteroom before Pilate's court. Caiphas and Annas
enter. Procula, Pilate's wife, who is standing by, is sexy,
randy.)*

29

CAIPHAS: To thee, Pontius Pilate,
    The royalest ruler of rank and renown,
    Right Roman regent to rule this region in rest,
    We bow. To thy bidding we bishops are bound
    As bold men in battle who meet breast to breast.

PROCULA: Husband, of all womankind am I witty
    and wise?

PILATE: That may ye say safely; I will certify the
    same.

PROCULA: Dear Pilate, thank you, your praise most
    I prize.

PILATE: And to solace my soul I must kiss my dame.

PROCULA: To fulfill your fancy, my fair lord, I arise.

*(They kiss. The others discreetly clear their throats.
Pilate looks up.)*

PILATE: Come now, we wait on your need
    Either, sirs, of blight or debate
    That needs to be handled with speed,
    Since in my hand hangs all your fate.

ANNAS: Yea, sir; there is a rank swain
    Whose rule is not right....

PILATE: I hear well ye hate him, and wildly are
    wroth.
    Be ready, array forth your reason.

CAIPHAS: For he teaches folk for him to call
    Great God's son; it is nought but treason.

PROCULA: Do hark how they prate and prattle,
    these two.
    Just go beat that whore's son, thus do I bid thee.

CAIPHAS: But Madame, we do only what we can do.

30

PROCULA: Pfah. If thou wait for a reason, sorry
you'll be;
You are but fearful this slave to subdue.

PILATE: Hold, madam, and your mood amend.
For me seems it suitable to see what he says.

ANNAS: My Lord, with false witchcraft the people
this Jesus blinds!

PILATE: Yes?

ANNAS: Our laws he will defy.

PILATE: Yes?

CAIPHAS: He worketh false miracles of all kinds.

PILATE: Yes?

ANNAS: Yea, sir; and also this Christ,
He calls himself our king.

PILATE: What!

ANNAS: Ruler of us all.

PILATE: If so be, that boast to break him will bring,
And make him to curse the clubs that him clout.

(Christ and the disciples before Simon's house)

SIMON: Wondrous Lord, welcome thou be!
Reverence receive thee, both God and man
My poor place I proffer free
Simply to serve thee as I can.

JESUS: Simon, I trust thy true intent.
The height of heaven have thou secured.
This reward to thee I do present,
There is joy of joys for thee assured.

*(Christ enters the house with his disciples and eats the
Pascal Lamb. Mary Magdalen approaches Christ.)*

31

MAGDALEN: Have mercy, Lord, and my wounds
    bind.
Mary Magdalen is my name.
Sordid sinner, scorned by all mankind;
So steeped in sin; of such ill fame.
I have befouled in forest and marsh
And sought sin in many a city.
Unless you save me, my fate, harsh:
In hell ever to punished be.

JESUS: Woman, now thy weeping still.
Some comfort God to thee shall send,
Thee to save, such is my will,
For sorrowful heart does sin amend,
All thy prayer I shall fulfill;
To thy good heart I will attend
And save thee from thy sins so ill,
From seven devils I shall thee defend.

(he conjures out of her the seven deadly sins)

Fiends, fly away!
Wicked spirits, I you conjure,
Fly out of her body's bower!
In my grace she shall ever flower
Till death take her away.

My heart is right sorry—and no wonder is—
To death I shall go, yet never have I sinned.

But yet most grieveth my heart ever of this;
One of you here will betray me; 'tis destined.

PETER: My dear Lord, I pray thee the truth for to
    tell;
Which of us he that treason shall do?

BARTHOLOMEW: Dear Lord, tell us his name, this
    traitor loseth his soul.
Damned shall he be for his damnable goal.

THOMAS: Rest shall he have none, but evermore
    wake.

For this terrible deed, the devil him shall take.

*(when it is Judas's turn to talk, Lucifer, unseen by those
present, suddenly appears at his elbow)*

JUDAS: The truth would I know as well as ye;
    And therefore, good sir, the truth thou me tell,
    Which of us all here that traitor may be;
    Am I, Judas, that person that thee now shall
    sell?

JESUS: Those are your words. Heed what thou now
    say.
    Thou askest me now here if thou shalt do that
    treason.
    Now question thyself; think thee on thy way,
    Thou art mature and know thine own reason.

*(Now Lucifer rises and Judas immediately rises, too.
With Lucifer leading the way, they leave the supper. The
lights go out on the supper scene—or a curtain is
drawn—leaving Judas and Lucifer alone.)*

JUDAS: Now well devised, I have a secret treason,
    My master's power to overthrow;
    For this he has given me ample reason
    He would us straight to heaven's glory go,
    Neglect on earth the deep, sad misery of man.
    I Judas shall, the first time that I can,
    Him betray to Pilate. Now I go.

(Lucifer nods approvingly and leads the way)

(Pilate's court)

PILATE: If then this Christ calls himself king,
    Go get him that we may examine this thing.

ANNAS: I know him not, only that he is clad in a
    cape,

That his is a keen face, his mouth e'er agape.

(Judas is marched in by a guard. Lucifer is behind him.)

GUARD: *(to Judas)* Come on lively now to my lord,
    listen, you lout.
    When utter you language then short shall you
    sing.

JUDAS: Hail princes and prelates that are present!
    New tidings to you I come to say,
    If you will trust to my intent;
    My master Christ I would betray,
    For I will no farther follow his way.

PILATE: What are you called?

JUDAS: Judas Iscariot.

PILATE: By whom were you sent?

JUDAS: Of my own will did I decide.

PILATE: Thou art a just man, but will Jesus be
    justified
    By our judgment?

ANNAS: Here are thirty pieces of silver bright
    Securely sealed in this glove.
    Set us to seize thy master tonight,
    This shalt thou have, and all our love.

JUDAS: Ye are reasonable men, this suits me well.
    This bargain between us shall I make;
    'Tis done. There's nothing more to tell.
    Him I will forsake.

CAIPHAS: But sir, how so shall we him know,
    For each disciple is like your master in his dress?

JUDAS: With soldiers set to seize him go,
    I shall mark him so you shall not miss;

When you circle us all about,
Take the man that I shall kiss.

PILATE: This plan is good, I have no doubt.

JUDAS: I go.

PILATE: Abide in my blessing and bring forth thy
best.

(They leave. Pilate kisses Procula.)

PILATE: Let us to bed. There is devotion discovered.

PROCULA: And there, sir, what is it you'd have?

PILATE: All ladies, we covet them to be kissed and
uncovered.

*(Judas walks back as the lights go out on the scene.
Lucifer walks with him a little way, then stops and
watches him go off.)*

LUCIFER: Ah. Ah, Judas, darling mine,
Thou art the best ever brought to me by fate.
Thou has sold thy master and all now is fine.
This Jesus his death we now await.

(Lucifer goes off in another direction)

*(Jesus, followed by his disciples, goes to the Mount
of Olives)*

JESUS: This night from you be led I shall,
And ye for fear from me shall flee—
Nor dare you speak when I you call—
And some of you forsake me.

For you I shall die and rise again;
Then on the third day ye shall me see
Before you all, walking plain
In the land of Galilee.

PETER: Lord, I will thee never forsake,

Nor for no perils from thee flee.
I will rather my death take
Than once, Lord, forsake thee.

JESUS: Peter, thou sayest more than thou dost
know.
Take care, that promise thou shouldst not make;
For ere twice more the cock doth crow
Thrice thou shall me forsake.
The time is come, the day draweth near;
Unto my death I must in haste.

JESUS: Peter, with thy fellows here shalt thou abide
And watch till I come again.
I must make my prayers here, you aside.
My flesh quaketh sore for fear and pain.

(Jesus moves off from the others and prays)

JESUS: O Father, Father! for my sake
This pitiless pain please take from me,
Which is decreed that I shall take
If mankind's souls saved may be.
And if my fate, Father, is to be,
To save man's souls from certain hell,
I follow fast, in full degree,
Thy will as to me ye did tell.

But Father in heaven, I beseech thee,
Spare me my pain by thy great grace,
And let me from this death flee,
Since I did never no trespass!
The water and blood drips from my face,
Drips for pain that I shall take;
My flesh quaketh in fear apace
As though the joints asunder should shake.

(here Gabriel comes to Jesus and brings him a chalice)

GABRIEL: Hail, both God and man so dear!
Thy father has sent thee this present.

36

He bade thou shouldst not fear.
But fulfill his intent.

This chalice is thy blood, this bread is thy body.
For man's sin ever offered be;
To the father of heaven that is almighty,
Thy disciples and all priesthood shall offer
  before thee.

(the angel exits)

JESUS: Father, thy will fulfilled shall be.

(Jesus walks to his disciples. An armed band appears and confronts them. Judas and Lucifer are with the band.)

JESUS: Sirs, ye push into this place
  To find him that will not flee.
  We fear you not. Now do me face
  And tell me whom seek ye.

KNIGHT 1: Whom we seek here I tell thee who:
  A traitor, who's worthy to suffer death.
  We know he is here among you;
  His name is Jesus of Nazareth.

(Judas comes forward)

JUDAS: All hail, master, in faith. And fellows all
    here.
  With gracious greeting this ground be arrayed.
  I would ask you a kiss, master, if you will.

JESUS: Full heartily, Judas, have it even here.
  With this kissing is Man's son betrayed.

  Sirs, I am here that will not flee,
  Do to me all that you can.
  In truth I tell you I am he,
  Jesus of Nazareth, that same man.

37

(Here all the soldiers suddenly fall rigid to the ground. Jesus gives a sign and they rise again.)

(Jesus is taken. Lucifer disguised.)

LUCIFER: All is ready. The cross that he shall die
    upon is done,
    And three nails to hold him so he shall not
    move.
    Be he holiest of holy he'll not from me run,
    But rather with his death my power prove.

    Then after he shall come to hell, his pretensions
    done.
    The chains that bind him will his story disprove.

    Judas, is it?

JUDAS: Yes.

LUCIFER: I hear that thy master is taken.
    Your freedom now must great joy bring.

JUDAS: Not so, sir. By his Father, Jesus' fate was
    written.
    Someone was destined to do this thing.

LUCIFER: How say you, Judas! Have not Christ and
    his Father lost their game?

JUDAS: Nay, sir, not so.
    We disciples know.
    God's son is he,
    Sent to die, man to free
    From Adam's blame.

LUCIFER: Surely thou jest. *(aside)* This pleaseth me
    in no way.
    (to Judas) Why was he then betrayed by one who
    knew his fate was to betray?

JUDAS: It lies in each man's choice, to destiny obey.

LUCIFER: *(aside)* This answer pleaseth me not.
(to Judas) But surely, Christ now goes to hell.

JUDAS: Yes. As did his Father plan and plot,
And once Christ is in hell, Satan will fall as he
once fell.
So it is planned.

LUCIFER: Then he will in hell, Satan's power break?

JUDAS: So it is planned.

LUCIFER: Then he will in hell Satan's power take?

JUDAS: So it is planned.

LUCIFER: It was so planned from the beginning?

JUDAS: From the beginning.

LUCIFER: Thank you, good sir. I shall not keep thee
more.

(Judas exits)

LUCIFER: *(realizing he has blundered)*
O! O! I see 'tis not as it did seem.
My pretty plan its opposite did spawn.
I had no thought when I did scheme,
That Lucifer in God's design was but a pawn!
This day goes worse than I did dream.
I must say my game seems gone.

Wait! If quickly I do act,
And Jesus' life I save somehow.
Hell's gates ever stand intact,
Mankind to me shall ever bow.

To Pilate's wife I will now go
As she is asleep in bed full fast,
And in her mind the thought I'll sow
To Pilate she shall bring in haste.

(Here the devil goes to Pilate's wife. Soon after he comes in, she makes a rueful noise, awakening and running before Pilate like a mad woman.)

PILATE'S WIFE: A fiend brought to my bed 'ere morn
Such troubled thought as I slept fast;
Since the time that I was born
Was I never so sore aghast.
Pilate I plead with my last breath,
Damn not Jesus, but be his friend.
If thou doom him to dismal death,
Thou art damned forever without end.

PILATE: *(patronizing)* Thank you, my good wife,
forever ye be true.
And your counsel welcome as always it be.
Now to your bedroom back go you
And all shall be well, dame, as ye shall see.

(Jesus is brought before Pilate. Knights. High priests. Lucifer lurking.)

PILATE: Speak, and excuse thee, if thou can.

JESUS: Every man has a mouth that is his to mold,
In wealth and in woe at his will to wield.
If he govern it goodly, just as God told,
Then his spiritual speech shall not to sin yield.
And such man as speaketh so ill,
Shall rue it and ill shall he reap.
For each tale that you tell us, you will
Account for it. A lie cannot keep.

PILATE: Jesus, I understand thou art a king
And the son of God art thou also.

JESUS: If you would know this thing
To heaven and my Father go.

PILATE: Sirs mine,
I find, in his faith is no feign;

40

For in this lad no lies are plain,
Nor no point to put him to pain.

CAIPHAS: Not so, sir; for now, as ye know,
To be king he claimeth with crown.

PILATE: Sir, truly that touches to treason,
And ere I go he shall right rue that reason.

(to Jesus) Hark, fellow, come near.
Thou knowest I have the power
To forgive or decree here, to torment or forgive.

JESUS: Such power hast thou nought to work thy
will thus with me.
But from my Father is that brought, one great
God in persons three.

PILATE: Sir knights that are comely, take this caitiff
in keeping;
Strike him with scourges and lash him full sore,
Wrest him and wring him till for woe is he
weeping,
And then bring him before us as he was before.

*(Lucifer, in vain, attempts to intercede. The knights
punch and beat Jesus, who falls.)*

KNIGHT 2: Just to annoy us, this knave he but naps.

(they raise him up and beat him)

KNIGHT 3: We'll stir him with sounds of our slaps.

(a crown of thorns is held aloft)

KNIGHT 1: Now because he our king did him call,
We'll kindly him crown with a briar.

KNIGHT 2: Yea, but first this purple and pall
And this worthy weed shall he wear.

KNIGHT 4: Now his brain bleeds. My sovereign,
Hail!

41

(They bring him to Pilate. Barabbas is there.)

PILATE: Well, bring him before us. Ah, he blushes
    all blue.
    I trust of his treason he'll tell us no more.
    Sirs, look here on high and ecce homo
    Thus beaten and bound and brought you before.

    Your custom it is on this feast day to free
    One felon who may from sentence go.
    Barabbas, hold up thy hand.
    For here at thy delivery thou may stand.
    Who shall it be?

CAIPHAS: Sir, for the solemnity of this holy day,
    That thief he shall go free away.

PILATE: Barabbas, then I dismiss thee,
    And give thee license to go free.

    Hear the judgment of Jesus, all those in this
    place,
    Crucify him on the cross, and on Calvary him
    kill.
    I condemn him this day to die in disgrace;
    Therefore hang him on high upon that high
    hill.

(Judas enters)

JUDAS: I have sinned and terrible treason done,
    A holy one have I betrayed for greed.
    Here is your money again, the whole sum,
    I sorrow at my dire deed.

PILATE: What is that to us. Consider now,
    Thou didst with us a covenant make.
    Thou soldest him to us as horse or cow,
    The consequence then must thou take.

*(Christ bearing his cross makes his way to Calvary
followed by soldiers. The three Marys are in a group.)*

MARY 1: Alas, the time and tide.
  Alas is come the day
  That once was specified.

MARY 2: Alas, how doleful is the way.
  To death they do him send.

JESUS: Daughters of Jerusalem, weep not for me.
  Turn home to town again, since you have seen
    this sight.
  It is my Father's will. That which is done is right.

KNIGHT 3: What the devil is this to say?
  How long shall we stand still?
  Go, hie you hence away,
  In the devil's name, down the hill.

KNIGHT 1: Ye know yourselves as well as I
  How lords and leaders of our law
  Have deeded doom—that this dolt shall die.

KNIGHT 2: Sir, since all their council well we saw,
  Since we are come to Calvary,
  We are all ready under law.
  That order filled shall be.

KNIGHT 3: Let's hear how we shall do,
  And go to it with a will.

KNIGHT 1: He must be dead—needs must—by noon.

KNIGHT 2: Then is good time that we begin.

KNIGHT 3: He shall be bound and taught full soon.

KNIGHT 4: With grief to him and all his kin.

  *(they spread the cross on the ground and prepare the
  hammer and nails)*

JESUS: Almighty God, my Father free.
  Let this cause be kept in mind.
  Thou bade I should obedient be

43

For Adam's fate I suffering find.
Here to perish I pledge me
From that sin for to save mankind.
And principally I beseech thee
That man from this may favor find;
From the fiend them defend,
And so their souls I save,
In world without end.
I care nought else to crave.

KNIGHT 1: Ha, hark, sir knights, in plight so bad,
Of Adam's kind his only thought.

KNIGHT 2: This warlock waxes worse than mad;
This doleful death he dreadeth nought.

(Jesus lays himself on the cross)

KNIGHT 3: Behold, himself has lain him down
In length and breadth as he should be.

KNIGHT 4: This traitor here tainted with his treason,
Go fast and fetter him ye three;
And since he claimeth kingship with crown.
Like a king have it shall he.

KNIGHT 1: Now to work. I shall not rest
Until his right hand's bound.

KNIGHT 2: Let's see who ties him best,
I'll loop his left hand round.

(they stretch Christ's limbs to the bores)

KNIGHT 3: Now knights, what next for this knave?

KNIGHT 4: For sure, I think, I hold this hand.

KNIGHT 1: Strike hard for him that would thee save.

(they begin nailing)

KNIGHT 2: Yes, here's a stud will stiffly stand!
Through bones and sinews find its way.

(he hands the nail to Knight 2, who looks at him, then hammers it in)

I have this work now well in hand. *(all laugh)*

KNIGHT 3: Say, sir, how fare we here,
The time flies fast away.

KNIGHT 2: It falls short a foot I fear,
So shrunk the sinews stay.

KNIGHT 3: I think the mark amiss be bored.

KNIGHT 4: Then must he suffer piteous pain.

KNIGHT 2: Why carp ye so? Tie on a cord
And tug him to, with sweat and strain.

(they tie a rope to Jesus' arm and stretch it until it reaches the hole)

KNIGHT 4: Yea, thou command us lightly as a lord!
Come, help to haul, or do you ail?

KNIGHT 2: Now surely that shall I do
(aside) As quickly as a snail.

(Knight 4 drives a nail into Jesus' right hand)

KNIGHT 4: And I shall tack him to
Full nimbly with a nail.

KNIGHT 1: Go we all four then to his feet
And soon our task is speedily done.

(Knight 3 pulls at Jesus' feet playfully)

KNIGHT 3: Let see if he can take a joke.
He should his Father now invoke.

KNIGHT 3: *(examining holes at bottom of cross)*
Tsk. This work is all unfit.
This hole here must be mended.

KNIGHT 4: Ah. No, man, just stretch him a bit.

(he attaches a rope to Christ's feet)

Pull. Our work is now soon ended.

(they pull down on the rope to reach the incorrectly bored hole)

KNIGHT 1: Lug on ye both. We near our goal.
It is no matter how he feels.
Now haul.

KNIGHT 3: Ah now! Here is the hole.

KNIGHT 4: Have done. Drive in that nail
So that no fault be found.

(Knight 1 hammers a nail through Jesus' feet. Knight 3 inspects the job.)

KNIGHT 3: Split are the sinews and veins. Skill doth
prevail.
Our job is done. Our work is sound.

KNIGHT 1: Now all his tricks bring him no gain.
Deceit shall be with suffering bought.

KNIGHT 3: I will go say to our sovereign
Of all this work how we have wrought.

KNIGHT 4: Nay sirs, another thing falls first to you
and me.
They bade we should him hang on height that
men might see.

KNIGHT 3: We know well so their words were,
But sir, that deed will do us ill.

KNIGHT 4: It does no good to gabble here.
This harlot hangs upon this hill.

(they try to lift the cross)

KNIGHT 4: Lift up! *(all lift the cross)*

KNIGHT 3: Watch out!

46

KNIGHT 2: Oh! Heave hard!

KNIGHT 1: From all this harm he should him save
If he were God.

KNIGHT 4: Devil take the knave!

KNIGHT 1: This cross and I must separate,
Or else my back in two will bend.

KNIGHT 4: Let it down. Your din's too great.
This work for us will never end.

KNIGHT 3: By Mohamed, I nearly swooned.
My shoulder's split, I swear.

KNIGHT 2: And now my manhood's ruined.
Such lifting I can't bear.

KNIGHT 3: Now lift again. Soon we'll be there.
Get a good grip and do it fast.

KNIGHT 2: Now lift! *(they pick up the cross)*

KNIGHT 1: Heave ho!

KNIGHT 4: He's in the air!

KNIGHT 3: Hold tight!

KNIGHT 2: What now?

KNIGHT 1: The worst is passed.

(they reach the top of the hill)

KNIGHT 4: Now raise him nimbly for the nonce,
And set him in this mortice here.
And let it drop, quickly, at once.
For sure his pain will have no peer.

KNIGHT 3: Heave up!

KNIGHT 2: Let drop so all his bones do break.

(they drop the base of the cross into the mortice with a jolt)

47

KNIGHT 1: *(to Jesus)* Sir, this work we have done now;
　Have you then any complaint?

KNIGHT 4: We pray you say us how
　You feel. Perhaps a little faint?

(all laugh)

JESUS: All men that walk by way or street,
　My suffering sore should be your gain.
　Behold my head, my hands and my feet,
　And fully feel my pitiful pain.
　(praying) My Father that all harm does heal,
　Forgive these men their wicked zeal.
　For they know not what they do.

KNIGHT 4: Hey, Hark! He jangles like a jay.

(They leave. The three Marys, John the Apostle, and others enter.)

(the following lines are sung)

ALL: Alas!

MARY: Alas, for my sweet son I say
　That dolefully to death is done.

ALL: Alas!

MARY: Alas, for full lovely thou lay
　In my womb, thou worthy one.

ALL: Alas!

MARY: Alas that I should see this sight.
　Of my son so seemly to see.

ALL: Alas!

MARY: Alas that this blossom so bright
　Untruly is tied to this tree.

(end of singing)

48

JESUS: Eloi, eloi!
My God, My God, full free.
Lama sabacthani
Why hast thou forsaken me.

My friends that me in faith do prize.
Now from your foes I fast defend.
On the third day I will arise
And so to heaven I shall ascend.
Then shall I come again,
To judge both good and ill,
For endless joy or pain;
That is my Father's will *(dies)*

(Song. During the song Christ's body is taken down and brought to the tomb. The captain stations soldiers around the tomb.)

SOLDIER 1: 'Tis the third day, we are soon done.

SOLDIER 2: He is not risen. The day is won.

SOLDIER 3: We have kept him to our renown.
On every side let us sit down.
And surely we shall crack his crown
Who e're comes near.

(Jesus rises. The soldiers fall into a stupor. He pushes the stone aside.)

JESUS: My Father me from bliss did send
To earth for mankind's sake,
Adam's sin for to amend
My death need must I take.

Therefore till hell will I now go
To claim that which is mine.
Adam, Eve, and others more
No longer suffer pain and pine.

(the Marys approach the tomb)

49

GABRIEL: Ye women mourning in your thought,
Here in this place whom have ye sought?

MARY 1: Jesus, that unto death was brought.

GABRIEL: He is not here, the truth to say,
The place is void that he in lay.
He is risen.

(Jesus arrives at the gate of hell)

And now I will that place restore
Which the fiend fell from for sin.
Some token I will send before
With this sign their pleasures begin.

A light I will they have
To know I will come soon.

(in hell a glorious light shines)

ISAAC: Adam through thy sin
Here were we put to dwell,
This wicked place within;
The name of it is hell.

ADAM: My brethren, hearken to me here.
More hope of help we never had.
In the four thousand and six hundred year
We have been here in darkness sad.
Here's glorious gleam to make us glad,
Through which I hope that help is near.

EVE: Adam, my husband,
This means solace sure.
Such light's from heaven grand,
From paradise so pure.

NOAH: Here pain shall never cease
For the wicked and the cruel.
Love that lord of peace
Whose death is our renewal.

ISAAC: And that light here see we now
Shining on us certain
Will, truly, I vow,
Lead us to pass from this pain.

*(Jesus knocks at the gate, each knock a thunderclap.
The devil Ribald strives frantically to raise the alarm.)*

BEELZEBUB: Since first that hell was made and I was
put therein,
Such sorrow have I never had, nor heard I such
a din!
I dread we now shall surely lose these souls that
we did win.
Help, Lucifer! Such hubbub was never heard in
hell.

(Lucifer comes running)

LUCIFER: Beelzebub thou roarest! What the cause?

BEELZEBUB: Canst thou not tell?
These louts that now in limbo slave,
They cry on Christ full well
And say he shall them save.

LUCIFER: Ha, he'll have them not. I shall.
For they are shut in special space.
While I am prince and principal
They shall never pass out of this place.

(Jesus knocks on hell's gates)

JESUS: Attolite portas principes
Ye princes of hell open your gate
And let my people pass.

BEELZEBUB: What are thou that speakest so?

JESUS: A king of bliss, by name, Jesus.

BEELZEBUB: It is the Jew that Judas sold,
Doomed to be dead yet here this day....

LUCIFER: How? In time that tale is told
That traitor thwarts us in every way.
We'll lock him in our deepest hold.
See that he not escape, I say.

JESUS: Whether ye will or no,
A prince of peace shall enter here.

LUCIFER: Now fear him not we must
But boldly arm ye now
With weapons that you trust,
And lay the liar low.

BEELZEBUB: To drag him down is ready said.
Come thou thyself. Come, go ahead.
And take away his crown.

LUCIFER: Fie fickle traitor filled with fear.
Have ye no force to face our foe.
Go swiftly to prepare my gear.
Myself shall to that gadling go.

JESUS: This place shall no more unclosed be.
Open up and let my people pass.

(hell's gates burst open)

BEELZEBUB: Oh no. A terrible thing to see.
Our great gates are gone. Alas!
Limbo is lorn.
Lucifer, 'tis thy work.
Thy burden have we born.

(Lucifer marches to confront Jesus)

LUCIFER: Well, fair friend, we meet again.
I hear ye claim as thine
The mastery over wretched men
Whom I hold fast, forever mine.

JESUS: No mastery, thy wardship's filled.
They have here abided long—not as thine

52

But in thy keeping, as God willed.
Now saved by me as his design.

LUCIFER: Oh? Man has sinned four thousand year,
Yet never came ye near before.

JESUS: Now is that time here
My Father ordained therefore.
They pass from pain to cheer
In bliss to dwell forevermore.

LUCIFER: Thy father I knew well by sight
A carpenter by trade was he.
Let's see, Mary—your mother's name, right?
A simple shepherd's daughter, she.
So much for thy noble family.

JESUS: Thou wicked fiend. Let thy din end.
My Father dwells in heaven on high.
I am his only son, his will to tend.

LUCIFER: God's son?
Bel ami. Slain must thou be.

(*Jesus calls on his angels*)

JESUS: Michael, my angel, hither soon,
Fasten yon fiend that he not flee.
And devil, I command thee, go down
Into thy cell where thou shalt stay.

BEELZEBUB: Satan, this said we ere.
Now shall we rue our way.

LUCIFER: Alas, with grief and care
I fall so deep this day.

(*The devil falls. Pilate hurries to the tomb.*)

SOLDIER 1: Sir Pilate.

PILATE: Speak.

SOLDIER 1: The prophet Jesus...

PILATE: Speak!

SOLDIER 1: He is truly risen and gone, to all our awe,
Despite our main and might.

PILATE: Then the devil himself may thee draw,
False, recreant knight.

SOLDIER 1: I tell thee, Pilate, the earth trembled, and as a man, began to speak.
The stone, that never stirred ere then asunder brake. The dead man rose.

PILATE: Yea, but if the dead man rose bodily,
That might be done through sorcery;
Therefore we set nothing thereby.
I did ordain, that on this day,
Though prophesy did so purvey,
He shall not rise.
Nor none shall spirit him away
In any wise.

KNIGHT 1: No living man could Jesus stop,
We were so frightened, every one,
When he put aside the stone.
We were so astonished we dare stir, none.
We did but drop.

PILATE: Then rose he by himself alone?

KNIGHT 1: Yea, sir.

PILATE: Sir knight, take heed and hearken what ye are to say
To every man, both night and day.
Ten thousand men in good array,
Who would you kill
With force of arms, bore Christ away
Against your will.
Thus shall ye say in every land.

54

And more on that same covenant,
A thousand pounds have you and your fellows
    in your hand,
To your reward.

Thus shall the truth be bought and sold,
And treason shall for truth be told.
Therefore in your hearts now hold
This counsel clean.
And fare ye well both young and old
Who here are seen.
This Christ of whom too much is told will
    disappear.
Of him we'll hear no more as if he'd never been.

(hell)

JESUS: Adam and all my friends now here,
    From all your foes come forth to me;
    Ye shall be set in solace clear
    Where ye shall never sorrows see.
    And Michael, my archangel dear,
    Receive these souls unto thee
    And lead them that they may appear
    In paradise to abide with me.

(song)

55

ELEPHANT PAPERBACKS

Literature and Letters
Stephen Vincent Benét, *John Brown's Body*, EL10
Isaiah Berlin, *The Hedgehog and the Fox*, EL21
Philip Callow, *Son and Lover: The Young D. H. Lawrence*, EL14
James Gould Cozzens, *Castaway*, EL6
James Gould Cozzens, *Men and Brethren*, EL3
Clarence Darrow, *Verdicts Out of Court*, EL2
Floyd Dell, *Intellectual Vagabondage*, EL13
Theodore Dreiser, *Best Short Stories*, EL1
Joseph Epstein, *Ambition*, EL7
André Gide, *Madeleine*, EL8
John Gross, *The Rise and Fall of the Man of Letters*, EL18
Irving Howe, *William Faulkner*, EL15
Aldous Huxley, *After Many a Summer Dies the Swan*, EL20
Aldous Huxley, *Ape and Essence*, EL19
Aldous Huxley, *Collected Short Stories*, EL17
Sinclair Lewis, *Selected Short Stories*, EL9
William L. O'Neill, ed., *Echoes of Revolt: The Masses,
    1911–1917*, EL5
Ramón J. Sender, *Seven Red Sundays*, EL11
Wilfrid Sheed, *Office Politics*, EL4
Tess Slesinger, *On Being Told That Her Second Husband Has
    Taken His First Lover, and Other Stories*, EL12
Thomas Wolfe, *The Hills Beyond*, EL16

Theatre and Drama
Robert Brustein, *Reimagining American Theatre*, EL410
Robert Brustein, *The Theatre of Revolt*, EL407
Irina and Igor Levin, *Working on the Play and the Role*, EL411
Plays for Performance:
    Aristophanes, *Lysistrata*, EL405
    Anton Chekhov, *The Seagull*, EL407
    Georges Feydeau, *Paradise Hotel*, EL403
    Henrik Ibsen, *Ghosts*, EL401
    Henrik Ibsen, *Hedda Gabler*, EL413
    Henrik Ibsen, *When We Dead Awaken*, EL408
    Heinrich von Kleist, *The Prince of Homburg*, EL402
    Christopher Marlowe, *Doctor Faustus*, EL404
    The Mysteries: Creation, EL412
    The Mysteries: The Passion, EL414
    Sophocles, *Electra*, EL415
    August Strindberg, *The Father*, EL406

ELEPHANT PAPERBACKS

American History and American Studies